THE EAST COAST
BED &
BREAKFAST
GUIDE

Maplewood Inn, Fair Haven, Vermont

NEW ENGLAND AND THE MID-ATLANTIC

Bed & Breakfast Guide

EAST   COAST

BY ROBERTA GARDNER,
NAOMI BLACK, AND TERRY BERGER

Photographs by George W. Gardner

DESIGNED AND PRODUCED BY ROBERT R. REID
AND TERRY BERGER

PRENTICE HALL

NEW YORK

COVER PHOTOGRAPH:
Sweetwater Farm, Glen Mills, Pennsylvania

FRONTISPIECE PHOTOGRAPH:
Guest-room at Columns by-the-Sea, Cape May, New Jersey.

Editorial assistance by Michael Bingham.
Map by Anthony St. Aubyn.
Photograph on page 83 by Will Faller.
Photograph on page 82 courtesy of the Manor House.

Published by Prentice Hall Trade Division
A Division of Simon & Schuster, Inc.
Gulf + Western Building
One Gulf + Western Plaza
New York, New York 10023

A Robert Reid/Terry Berger production
Typeset in Bodoni Book by Monotype Composition Company, Baltimore
Produced by Mandarin Offset, Hong Kong

1 2 3 4 5 6 7 8 9 10

Library of Congress Cataloging-in-Publication Data

Gardner, Roberta Homan.
    East Coast bed & breakfast guide: New England and the mid
-Atlantic / by Roberta Gardner, Naomi Black, and Terry Berger;
photographs by George W. Gardner. — Completely updated, new ed.
      p.   cm.
   ISBN 0-13-072406-8 : $13.95
   1. Bed and breakfast accommodations—New England—Guide-books.
2. Bed and breakfast accommodations—Middle Atlantic States—Guide
-books.   I. Black, Naomi, 1957- . II. Berger, Terry.
III. Title.   IV. Title: East Coast bed and breakfast guide.
TX907.3.N35G37   1989
647'.947403—dc19   88-31869
                                   CIP

CONTENTS

continued overleaf

PENNSYLVANIA

NEW JERSEY

MARYLAND

WASHINGTON, D.C.

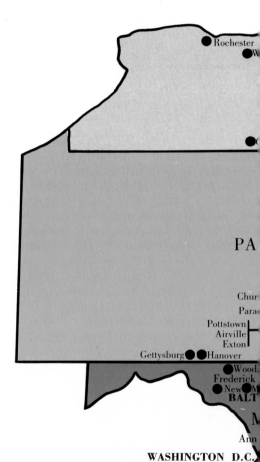

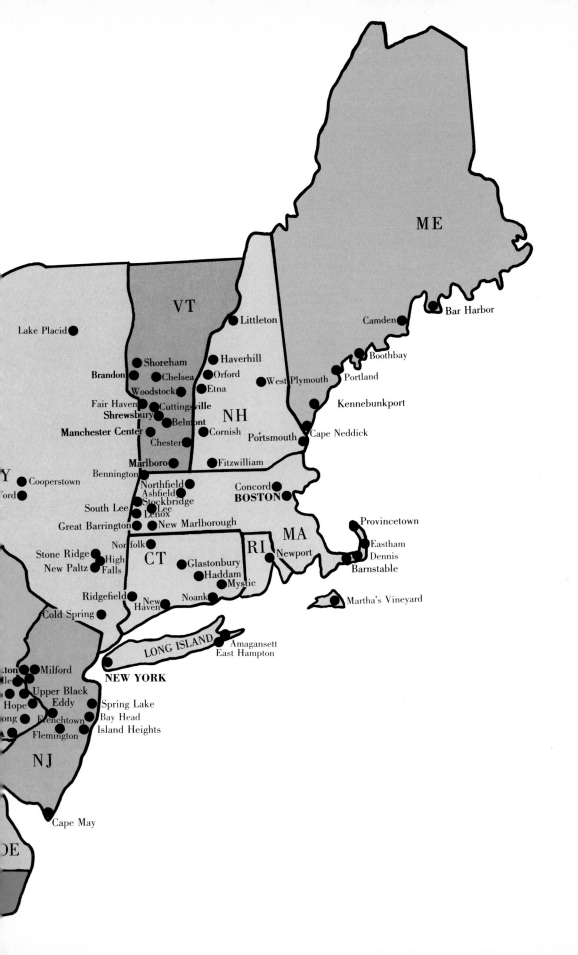

MAINE

Preserves the mood of Victorian gentility

James Blair built his summer home, a modest thirty-three room cottage, high on a rocky ledge overlooking the beautiful isle of Bar Harbor. His winter home in Washington, D.C., later used as an alternate presidential residence known as Blair House, sat across from the White House. Today both homes welcome travelers, Blair House serving as a home to dignitaries visiting the United States. Cleftstone Manor, under the thoughtful ownership of Phyllis and Donald Jackson, is a supremely lovely bed and breakfast inn.

The entire house is furnished with fine antiques, including such unusual pieces as Joseph Pulitzer's awesome writing table. This grand table amply fills the formal dining room and is put to use each day when it is laden with scones and shortbread at tea time and with cheeses and wine in the evening. Breakfast is served on the enclosed sunporch, a light-washed room complemented by white wicker furniture, a collection of Delft china, and masses of greenery.

The bedrooms, each different, are decorated with a confident and sophisticated touch. A favorite for honeymooners is the spacious Romeo and Juliet Room. One corner is given over to a brass canopied bed, draped in white lace. A comfortable love seat faces a working fireplace and the beautifully detailed coffered ceiling deepens the prevailing sense of privacy and luxury. The Glastonbury Room, with high-back Victorian bedstead, red velvet chair, hand-crocheted bedspread, and many decorative grace notes is serene.

CLEFTSTONE MANOR, Eden St., Bar Harbor, ME 04609; (207) 288-4951; Phyllis and Donald Jackson and family, hosts. Open May 15 to Oct. 15. Thirteen double rooms, three suites, four with fireplaces, three with balconies; mostly private baths. Rates: $75 double, shared baths, $85 to $150, private baths; rates include breakfast buffet with emphasis on home baking. Evening wine and cheese. Numerous restaurants nearby. Children over 12 welcome; no pets; Visa/MasterCard/American Express. The Jacksons are also proprietors of the nearby Tides Mansion, an ocean front estate.

DIRECTIONS: from points south, take Rte. 1 north to Ellsworth, then follow Rte. 3 into Bar Harbor. Inn is 500 feet past Bluenose Ferry terminal.

Left, the Romeo and Juliet honeymoon suite. Above, Joseph Pulitzer's writing table in the formal dining room.

NORUMBEGA

An extraordinary stone mansion

Norumbega is an extraordinary stone mansion whose elusive exterior seems to change when viewed at different angles. Designed by A.B. Jennings of New York City, the Queen Anne style manse is quite unique. From one angle the house shows a wall of roughly faced cobblestones, punctuated by arched windows and a rounded, stepped roof. From another, it resembles a more common seaside cottage with a wide porch and bay windows. Looking at the entrance, the *porte cochere*, and turret, the structure appears to be predominantly wood and brick. Close inspection

reveals at least three different shingle patterns on the turret, the name "Norumbega" and "1886" tiled and set in the right bay, and fossils embedded in the stone to the left of the entrance.

Inside, the wood draws first notice. Triangular-sawn oak with a marked sheen forms the entryway and three stairs to a landing with fireplace and elaborately carved corner seating. Spiral spindles below the banister add a suitably delicate touch.

The double parlors and curved study boast their share of beautiful wood. Carved grotesques, as compelling as Notre Dame's gargoyles, flank the fireplace; a central wood carpet establishes the floor theme.

Norumbega's eccentricities are attributable to its creator, Joseph Stearns, an inventor who made his fortune by patenting the "duplex system," a system by which two messages could be relayed by telegraph simultaneously.

Stearns was a man ahead of his time. He commissioned an astronomical observatory (now gone), a room to hold one hundred tons of coal, and a darkroom. The house, now restored to its full elegance, is a stunning home complete with mountain and water views. Murray and Elisabeth Keatinge, the new owners, afford gracious service and warm hospitality.

NORUMBEGA, 61 High St., Camden, ME 04843; (207) 236-4646; Murray and Elisabeth Keatinge, hosts. Open all year. Seven guest rooms, all with private baths, three with working fireplaces. Rates: $130 to $180; additional person, $50; includes generous, full breakfast. Children over 7 welcome; no pets; smoking permitted; all credit cards. Hiking, skiing, tennis, golf, ocean beach and freshwater lake, windjammer cruises, Lighthouse Museum in Rockland. Good restaurants.

DIRECTIONS: follow Rte. 1 north through Camden. The inn is on the right about one mile from town.

Left, the original reception hall. Above, a light and airy guest room.

Beamed ceilings and a 200-year-old cherry mantel.

KENNISTON HILL INN

Once a country club

The seventeen-mile-long Boothbay Peninsula extends into the ocean like a three-pronged fork, defined on either side by the Sheepscot and Damariscotta rivers. Newagen, one of the more established enclaves of seaside Maine, forms the point of the west tine. Ocean Point, with its scenic views, perches at the eastern tip in territory once frequented by Captain Kidd. The lively tourist haven of Boothbay Harbor lies in the middle.

A mile from the harbor, Kenniston Hill stands back from the street at the end of a narrow allé of maple and oak trees. This center-chimney colonial dates from 1786 when the prosperous Kenniston family moved in and established residence for almost a hundred years. The next notable owner acquired the house in 1922 and developed it as a clubhouse for the new Boothbay Country Club which still owns grounds adjacent to Kenniston Hill. After a brief time as an apartment house, the gracious building became an inn in 1956.

History helps make the inn a special place. Three separate entrances from its days as an apartment house add a welcome bit of privacy. Still, guests often choose to gather in front of the living room fireplace. The three-hundred-year-old cherry mantelpiece forms a nesting place for wooden ducks and assorted baskets. A collection of handmade and acquired stained glass light-catchers decorate the paned window wall.

Paul and Ellen Morisette retired to Kenniston Hill, giving up their Country Kitchen restaurant in Brattleboro, Vermont. "It's never humid here like Vermont. We don't need air conditioning. The windows are always open for breezes," Ellen says happily, "and now we have time to talk to people." They also have time to prepare an outstanding breakfast of such fare as delicately sauced eggs Benedict, fresh asparagus, and fluffy light popovers. Artfully presented fresh fruit pleases the eye as well as the palate.

The breakfast room, like most of the house, is furnished simply in deference to the colonial tradition. Pale yellow pineapple paper picks up the soft specks of gold and brown in the braided rug and the tawny hues of the pine sideboard. What makes Kenniston Hill most appealing, though, are the four guest rooms with working fireplace. A modest idyll, Kenniston Hill is perfect for all-season beachcombers and high-season sailors.

KENNISTON HILL INN, Rte. 27, Boothbay, ME 04537; (207) 633-2159; Paul and Ellen Morissette, hosts. Open April through November. White clapboard colonial built in 1786, on 4½ acres. Eight guest rooms, four with working fireplaces, all with private baths. Rates: $60 to $80, double; $10 for additional person. Full breakfast served. Children over ten preferred; no pets; MasterCard/Visa. Bicycles available at no charge; 9-hole golf nearby. Varied dining at the harbor.

DIRECTIONS: from Rte. 1 turn onto Rte. 27 south to Boothbay. The inn is on a knoll on the left.

ENGLISH MEADOWS INN

Like a visit to Grandma's

Gene Kelly bought Gussie English's country boarding house with a mind to renting out a room or two for a little extra income. Never in his wildest dreams did he imagine the devoted following that English Meadows Inn would inspire.

The inn sits on rolling and wooded acreage that still feels like country, though today the property dovetails with Kennebunkport's commercial center. Century-old lilacs, which perform gorgeously and fragrantly each spring, provide a curtain of privacy for the inn. Rooms in the main house are filled with antiques, rag and hooked rugs, and beautiful old patchwork quilts. Additional guest quarters in the adjoining rustic barn combine knotty pine, an open fireplace, wicker furniture, and views of field and garden to create a comfortable camplike atmosphere.

Behind the inn, and nestled in a pine grove, is an "enchanted" cottage. With its own full kitchen, dining room, and bedroom, it offers perfect solitude.

Breakfast prepared by Claudia is ample and delicious. One guest was so enamored of her sour dough French toast and maple syrup that he changed clothes, donned dark glasses, and seated himself for a second round. The poor fellow was found out, but the compliment was appreciated nonetheless.

Buttons, the inn's shaggy top dog, completes the scene and occasionally upstages Gene and Claudia, whose mutual senses of humor defy succinct description. Suffice it to say, Archie Bunker could take lessons from Gene.

ENGLISH MEADOWS INN, R.F.D. #1, Rte. 35, Kennebunkport, ME 04046; (207) 967-5766; Gene Kelly and Claudia Kelly Butler, hosts. A stay at this *circa* 1860 Victorian farmhouse is like a visit to Grandma's. Open April 1 through October, and weekends all year. Fourteen guest rooms with semi-private baths; two apartments; Enchanted Cottage. Rates: $45 to $55 single, $72 to $77 double, varying seasonally; apartments and cottage $700 per week, $110 per night, monthly rates available; rates include "famous" breakfast. Excellent dining nearby, especially seafood. No children under twelve; no pets; no credit cards. Maine coast is vacationer's dream for recreation, scenery, historic sites.

DIRECTIONS: take Maine Turnpike to exit 3 (Kennebunk). Turn left on Rte. 35 south. Inn is five miles ahead on right.

Guests like to make themselves at home in the living room.

INN AT HARBOR HEAD

Right on Maine's lobster coast

Artistry, elegance, and natural beauty in equal measure are the prime qualities of life at the Inn at Harbor Head. This intimate bed and breakfast is located on Kennebunkport's Cape Porpoise Bay, an idyllic lobstering cove whose sparkling waters are dotted with bobbing boats, rocky islands, and lighthouses that twinkle in the distance. Joan and Dave Sutter own the inn, a turn-of-the-century, weathered-shingle home that rambles along a promontory overlooking a sheltered harbor and the bay beyond.

Inside, the Sutters have created an elegant world that is sophisticated enough for the pages of a stylish home magazine. The inn's common rooms are furnished in a refined style, the living room displaying a crystal chandelier, a handsome Japanese screen, fine oriental rugs, and softly-lit oil paintings of the Sutters' ancestors. But real artistry is revealed in the four guest bedrooms. Joan is a seasoned artist—or, in her words, "a

Left above, the manicured lawn sweeps down to a private dock. Below, The Greenery is filled with morning light.

former three-dimensional artist now changed to 'wall painter' "—whose genius for color and design is wedded to an equally accomplished technical skill. Each bedroom plays out a romantic theme embellished by Joan's lyrical, painted imaginings inspired by the bay and surrounding village. The walls and ceiling of the Harbor Suite, for example, are decorated with soft and expressive murals that picture sailboats gliding across azure water; white herons stalking food in a shallow marsh; billowing white clouds on a field of soft blue; and a mother bird feeding eager fledglings.

The Sutters pamper their guests at breakfasttime, serving fresh-squeezed orange juice and fresh fruits, savory entrées, and fresh-baked breads. All may be savored amid the cut crystal and antique pewter in the dining room, or on the patio overlooking the water.

THE INN AT HARBOR HEAD, Pier Road, Cape Porpoise, RR 2, Box 1180, Kennebunkport, ME 04046; (207) 967-5564; Dave and Joan Sutter, hosts. Open all year, except for 2 weeks in the spring and Nov. Four rooms with private baths. Rates: $95 to $130, with full gourmet breakfast. Children over 12 welcome; no pets; Visa/MasterCard; a little Japanese spoken. Swimming from inn's dock. Whale watching, art galleries, summer theater, antiquing in area. Every style of dining available nearby.

DIRECTIONS: from Maine Turnpike take exit 3 and follow Rte. 9 east through Kennebunkport Village to Cape Porpoise. Leave Rte. 9 at Mobil station and take the road to the pier for ³/₁₀ miles to inn on right.

The Harbor Suite has hand-painted murals in both rooms.

Breakfast room in the main house.

OLD FORT INN

Kennebunkport charm

The Old Fort Inn is a charming carriage house-lodge combination that invites travelers for long-term stays. The fourteen color-coordinated American and English country-style rooms come with color television, extra bed, efficiency kitchens stocked with ironstone plates, wine glasses, pans, tea kettle, toaster, napkins and placemats—even laundry facilities.

It's one-and-a-half miles from the inn to town, an easy bike ride past lovely frame cottages and old sea captains' houses. Kennebunkport retains much of its late nineteenth-century atmosphere when ship building gave way to the tourist industry. Wealthy summer visitors built wisely and well, keeping the village quaint and relatively small. The inn's location, just a few blocks from the rocky shore, is also adjacent to Cape Arundel, where some of the most handsome turn-of-the-century cottages still stand.

Kennebunkport offers a rich variety of activities: trolley rides, scenic cruises, sailing lessons, yacht charters, and whale watching are but a few. The sports menu complements what the Old Fort Inn has to offer on its grounds. A swimming pool, shuffleboard area, and tennis court bridge the gap between the guest rooms and the main lodge where breakfast is served.

Sheila and David Aldrich and their daughter oversee the homemade muffins and fresh-baked breads for the continental breakfast. Friendships often begin at the morning meal and extend into the evening hours around the pool.

The Old Fort Inn presents the best of what casual adult resorts can provide: a relaxed atmosphere amid pleasant surroundings.

OLD FORT INN, Old Fort Ave., Kennebunkport, ME 04046; (207) 967-5353; Sheila and David Aldrich, hosts. Open April 26 to mid-December. Fourteen guest rooms plus two suites, all with private baths and efficiency kitchens. Rates: $86 to $125; suites, $135 to $185; additional person, $15. Rates include expanded continental breakfast and one hour of tennis daily. Children over 12 welcome; no pets; cigars and pipes in bedrooms only; pool on premises. American Express/MasterCard/Visa/Discover.

DIRECTIONS: take exit 3 (Kennebunkport) from the Maine Turnpike, then take a left on Rte. 35 and follow signs through Kennebunk to Kennebunkport. Take a left at the traffic light at the Sunoco station. Go over the drawbridge and take the first right onto Ocean Ave. Take Ocean Ave. to the Colony Hotel, turn left in front of the Colony, go to the Y in the road and take the right branch ¼ mile. The inn is on the left.

Each guest room has a kitchenette.

A spacious third-floor guest room

CAPTAIN JEFFERDS INN

A New England sea captain's house

The Kennebunkport historic district is peppered with gracious "cottages" built in the early 1800s by seafaring captains who traveled the globe in pursuit of treasure.

Warren Fitzsimmons and Don Kelly were partners in a successful antiques business when they bought one of these—Captain Jefferds' home—and brought the place to vibrant life. If, upon entering, you have a sense of déjà vu, don't doubt your feelings. The work of these two gifted innkeepers has been featured on the covers of several prestigious home decorating magazines. Two cobalt blue vases displaying a bounty of brilliant silk flowers flank the formal entryway. To the left is the breakfast room where guests gather each morning to be served by Don, dressed in butler's whites. Warren mans the kitchen, serving up custardy French toast, delicate pancakes, and perfectly turned eggs.

Each bedroom is special. Several are decorated in Laura Ashley's simple prints; others are dressed in muted tones that dramatize an elegant chaise, bird's-eye maple chest, or Chinese screen.

The collection of antiques in this inn is endlessly fascinating. Warren and Don buy only the truest examples of a representative period—there are no reproductions in the entire inn—and the place practically vibrates from the beauty produced by their combined collections. Though Warren and Don were personally attracted to American antiques, from tramp and shell art to twig furniture and Indian baskets, the inn's formal lines required sterling silver and crystal as well. It all works.

THE CAPTAIN JEFFERDS INN, Pearl St., Box 691, Kennebunkport, ME 04046; (207) 967-2311; Warren Fitzsimmons, host. 1804 Federal style sea captain's house. Open all year except closed during January, February, March. Twelve guest rooms in main house, all private baths; three efficiency apartments in carriage house. Rates $65 single, $75 to $95 double; apartments $550 per week, in season; guests in main house are treated to full breakfast, with seasonal specialties. No children under twelve; pets welcome, with advance notice; smoking not permitted in dining room; no credit cards.

DIRECTIONS: take Maine Turnpike to exit 3 to Rte. 35. Follow signs through Kennebunk to Kennebunkport. Turn left at traffic light and cross drawbridge. Turn right at monument onto Ocean Ave. Proceed 3/10 mile to Arundel Wharf and turn left onto Pearl St.

WOODEN GOOSE INN

A stunning restoration

Right off Route 1, sometimes called the "antique row of New England," the Wooden Goose Inn corners off its own country garden in full view of the Cape Neddick River. Guests gazing out from the glassed-in breakfast room overlook the perennial blooms and a specially commissioned Chippendale garden bench. The bench is just one of interior designer Jerry Rippetoe's unique additions to this intimate country house. Partner Tony Sienicki, the other half of this able team, attends to most of the carpentry and finishing.

The precision restoration began June 15, 1983, the day they bought the house. By July 2, after working twenty-two-hour days, Jerry and Tony welcomed their first overnight visitors. The quick revitalization succeeded only because of professional foresight and months of planning and preparation. "The day we looked at it we took measurements," remarked Tony.

The result is stunning. A true overabundance of Victorian paraphernalia blends with revitalized Orientalia. The focus in the reception room rests

on the hand-carved, hand-painted cormonde screen, a black lacquer on teak *chef-d'oeuvre* tha hints at other treasures inside. Guests are rarel disappointed with the many beautiful touches.

Excess and elegance are synonymous here Twenty-eight yards of chintz drape down from on canopy. The clawfoot tub of bedroom number stands in regal spaciousness next to a bentwoo rocker, a combination that inspires guests to brin their own bubble bath and champagne.

Morning starts with elaborate breakfasts serve on Lenox china with silver and linen asides. Plan to replace Sheelan crystal with Waterford illustrat the dynamics of the Wooden Goose. Every Januar the doors close for redecoration. Balloon shade change to miniblinds; greens give way to blues The transformation keeps the inn vital—and keep guests returning year after year.

THE WOODEN GOOSE INN, Rte. 1, Cape Neddick, ME 0390: (207) 363-5673; Tony Sienicki and Jerry Rippetoe, hosts. Ope February through December. Six guest rooms, all with priva baths. Rates: $85 to $95; suite, $130; including an elegan hearty breakfast which changes every day. Afternoon tea. Dinir nearby. Children over 12 welcome; no pets; no credit cards. Tl ocean is one mile from the inn. Golf, tennis, and bicycling Ogunquit.

DIRECTIONS: take I-95 to the York exit (No. 1, marked "la exit before toll"). Turn north on Rte. 1 for 3.4 miles. The in is on the right, five houses after the junction of Rtes. 1 and 1A

Third floor guest room decorated in a superb harmony of colors.

INN AT PARK SPRING

A city refuge for business or pleasure

The Inn at ParkSpring serves as an intimate home-away-from-home for visitors to the city of Portland. Conveniently located in the heart of this thriving and progressive community—walking distance to the Old Port shopping district, the newly renovated waterfront, the Portland Museum of Art, the Civic Center, and just ten minutes from the airport—this tailored townhouse bed and breakfast is the ideal base for both business and pleasure.

Innkeeper Wendy Wickstrom is the consummate concierge, providing small comforts and personalized service, including an afternoon tea-and-cookies pick-me-up, insider information on what to do and see in the city, and flexible check-in times.

The seven guest rooms are an eclectic collection, each decorated simply and tastefully. On the first floor one finds the Park Room, with its four-poster bed, formal marble fireplace, and crystal chandelier, juxtaposed with the Murphy Room, which sports an old-fashioned pull-down bed and a hide-a-bed sofa. The second floor houses two traditionally furnished bedrooms, one with a private balcony overlooking the newly gentrified historic district. Two third-floor bedrooms are tucked in the eaves and share a Swedish sauna-style cedar bathroom. Although both are uncluttered and simple, they vary in mood from contemporary Scandinavian to a cozy, rose-colored nook. Finally, back at ground level, the Courtyard Room has its own private entrance and courtyard.

THE INN AT PARK SPRING, 135 Spring Street, Portland, ME 04101; (207) 774-1059; Wendy Wickstrom, mgr.; Karen Angfendler, asst. mgr. Open all year. Seven rooms, 5 with private baths. Rates: vary seasonally from $65 to $85, with light breakfast. Children over 6 welcome; no pets; Visa/MasterCard/American Express. Fine arts museum around the corner; this historic old city has many fine restaurants for dining.

DIRECTIONS: from north or south on I-295 take exit 6A, bear right and turn right at light. Follow signs for Rte. 77 South through Deering Oaks Park. Stay in left lane and turn left at third light on to Congress St. (at Longfellow monument) and proceed 1 block and turn right on Park St. for 1 block to corner of Spring and Park.

NEW HAMPSHIRE

LEIGHTON INN

Colonial elegance n old Portsmouth

he elegance and refinement of the colonial period s showcased in the Leighton Inn, located within n easy walk of Portsmouth's historic Old Harbor. 'he house, a classic white clapboard finished ith Federal detailing, was built in 1809 and horoughly refurbished in the 1980s. Innkeeper Catherine Stone fell in love with the building's lean, strong lines, which she instantly knew ould harmonize with her collection of antique Empire furnishings. In combining the two, Catherine created a serene and inviting bed and reakfast inn, a peaceful haven filled with books, music, and flowers.

Furnishings and window treatments throughout he inn are in keeping with the colonial period. 'atherine researched authentic colonial colors as ell, and chose from that palette deep rose, butter ellow, rich blue, and mustard gold to accent ooms. She then furnished each simple and pristine bedroom with antiques from her extensive ollection.

Each morning Catherine treats guests to a enerous and leisurely breakfast which, in sum-

Above and on opposite page, superbly restored rooms, showing off the Empire furniture.

PHOTOGRAPH COURTESY LEIGHTON INN

mer, is savored on the screened-in porch, the better to enjoy the inn's fragrant perennials garden. Breakfast is hearty, and it includes juice and fresh fruit (including home-grown raspberries, in season); cinnamon blueberry or Scandinavian apple muffins, hot from the oven; herbed eggs; a breakfast meat; sautéed potatoes; and a hot beverage. Thus fortified, guests venture forth to discover the multi-layered personality of Portsmouth, which is redolent of history and filled with diverse and exciting restaurants and shops.

LEIGHTON INN, 69 Richards Avenue, Portsmouth, NH 03801; (603) 433-2188; Catherine Stone, host. Open all year. Five rooms with 4 baths. Rates: $50 to $75 double with full New England breakfast. Well-behaved children welcome; no pets; Visa/MasterCard; French, German spoken. 1913 Steinway available, bicycles for rental. Portsmouth is an historic city with many activities, including a summer arts festival and many fine restaurants.

DIRECTIONS: from I-95 take exit 5 to Portsmouth Traffic Circle and follow Rte. 1 Bypass North to Maplewood Ave. exit and turn right. Follow Maplewood into town, where its name changes to Middle St., which makes a broad curve to the right. Richards Ave. is first left after curve; inn is 6th house on left.

THE INN AT CHRISTIAN SHORE

Make yourself at home

The Inn at Christian Shore offers visitors to historic Portsmouth an opportunity to relax in one of the city's historic homes and partake of one of the grandest breakfasts anywhere.

After applying considerable energy and talent to the restoration of this sea captain's home, Louis Sochia, Thomas Towey, and Charles Litchfield opened their cozy and comfortable house to the public. The dining room is particularly charming with exposed beams, dark blue wainscoting, open fireplace, harvest table and Hitchcock chairs, and attractively displayed antique prints and primitive paintings.

Breakfast begins with juice or fresh fruit in season and a warm fruit loaf, possibly Tom's special banana-blueberry bread. Next, guests are served an egg dish and steak, pork tenderloin, or ham fried with pineapple. This substantial "main course" is always accompanied by home-fried potatoes and a vegetable in season—broccoli, cauliflower, or possibly steamed squash—a slice of tomato on a bed of lettuce, toast, and a hot beverage.

Though after such bounteous fare, food is not foremost in one's mind, Portsmouth offers an amazing array of wonderful restaurants. A short distance from the inn is the renowned Blue Strawberry, which is noted for skillfully prepared dishes created by a chef of rare talent and ingenuity.

THE INN AT CHRISTIAN SHORE, 335 Maplewood Ave., Portsmouth, NH 03801; (603) 431-6770; Charles Litchfield, Thomas Towey, and Louis Sochia, hosts. Sea captain's house, Federal style *circa* 1800. Open all year. Six guest rooms, including one single; private and shared baths. Rates: $30 single all year, $60 to $65 double, additional person $20, including exceptionally extravagant breakfast. Wine served in afternoon. Good restaurants within walking distance. Children over 12 welcome; no pets; no credit cards; personal checks accepted.

DIRECTIONS: from Boston, take I-95 to exit 5 and proceed to Portsmouth Rotary Circle. Drive halfway around to Rte. 1, proceeding north to Maplewood Ave. exit (last exit before bridge) and turn right. Inn is sixth house on left. Parking behind house.

Host Louis Sochia in the living room.

MOOSE MOUNTAIN LODGE

Casual, with lots of fireplaces

Moose Mountain Lodge virtually spills over the western slope of Moose Mountain. Porch-sitters recline in full view of unspoiled countryside, where Vermont's Green Mountains rise out of the clear, smooth-running waters of the Connecticut River.

Just a dozen or so miles northeast of Hanover, home of Dartmouth College, the lodge is a back-country hideaway on forty acres, situated on a dirt cul de sac that ends at the top of a ridge. Between the lodge and the mountaintop the road is veined with numerous trails, far away from the whoosh of passing traffic and noisy crowds. Winter skiers and summer hikers can disappear into the woods and feel secluded.

Inside, Kay and Peter Shumway cater to nature-lovers who gather around one of three common-room fireplaces. The stone fireplace in the living room warms-up conversation as much as it does noses and toes.

"You can put your feet up here. We love tracked-in snow!" says Kay, who emphasizes that her guests relax without thinking about ruining the floors or spilling a drink. Somehow, the Shumways still manage to keep the lodge fresh, clean, and comfortable.

After dinner many folks head down to the bar room (BYOB) to play ping-pong, darts, or a board game by yet another native stone fireplace, this one mottled with garnet-studded rose quartz. A working player piano livens up the evening with classic old favorites. Once the music's over, guests retire to appropriately rustic bedrooms made especially homey with handmade spruce log or other wooden beds and muted Marimekko linens.

MOOSE MOUNTAIN LODGE, Etna, NH 03750; (603) 643-3529; Kay and Peter Shumway, innkeepers. Open January to late March and June to November. Twelve cozy rooms share five modern bathrooms plus two tiled bathrooms in common rooms. Hearty breakfast. Rates: $40 per person. Dinners are offered year-round to guests only for an additional $15 per person. Children over 5 are welcome; no pets; no smoking. 50 km of cross-country ski trails; downhill skiing within 10 miles; hiking trails. Dartmouth College offers cultural events year-round.

DIRECTIONS: from exit 18 on Rte. 89, go north on Rte. 120 toward Hanover, ½ mile. Higbea Motel and Lander's Restaurant are on the left. Turn right here onto Etna Rd. into Etna Village. Go ½ mile past the Etna Store (phone from here if it's your first time) and turn right onto Rudsboro Rd. (just before the church. Go up Rudsboro Rd. 2 miles, then turn left on Dana Rd. Continue on Dana Rd. for ½ mile. Turn right. Drive up the mountain one mile to the Lodge.

WHITE GOOSE INN

Cozy American with European panache

Orford is seated by the banks of the upper Connecticut River just across a bridge from Fairlee, Vermont. Originally a "fort town" built by the British, it soon hummed with activity from logging and agriculture. Seven "ridge houses" dating from between 1773 and 1839 form a stately white row by the green in the town's center.

The White Goose Inn is also celebrated for its elm tree growing through the circular colonial revival porch. Manfred and Karin Wolf adopted this brick and woodframe home and transformed it into a cozy American country classic with European panache.

Karin, a craftsperson whose work is evident throughout the inn, did all the delicate stenciling, made the pierced parchment lampshades, and cunningly assembled traveler's sewing kits for each impeccably designed, spotless guest room.

White geese are the house motif. A porcelain goose with a pink satin ribbon around its neck sits in the window; a cloth goose pokes its head out of a basket on the hutch; and an early American metal cut-out depicts a young girl followed by two geese. And there's a white wooden goose on the marble-topped treadle sewing machine base in the hall to greet guests when they arrive.

Breakfasts are very special here, reflecting the hosts' European heritage. Hearty home-baked goods look even more tempting on the Wolf's fine china.

The tasteful choices in furnishing and accessories are consistent throughout the White Goose. The parlor exudes the glow from an unusual porcelain chandelier. The dining room benefits from a beautifully crafted modern wood table and tall Shaker-style chairs.

This wonderful hideaway engages its guests, tempting them again and again to relax and sit back in an attractive setting where the details in every room please the eye.

THE WHITE GOOSE INN, Rte. 10, P.O. Box 17, Orford, NH 03777; (603) 353-4812; Manfred and Karin Wolf. German spoken. Open all year. Sixteen guest rooms, most with private baths. Rates: $65 to $115, including a full country breakfast. Children under 8 discouraged; no pets; smoking discouraged. MasterCard/Visa. Hiking, biking trails, golf, skiing, sleigh rides; Saint-Gaudens National Historic Site. Dartmouth College, 15 miles.

DIRECTIONS: from I-91, take exit 15 (Fairlee, VT); cross the bridge to New Hampshire and take Rte. 10 south one mile. The inn is on the left. From I-93, take exit for I-89 and continue to Rte. 10 north. The inn is approximately 15 miles north of Hanover on the right.

Collecting maple syrup from the inn's own trees.

BIRTHPLACE OF
SALMON P. CHASE
JAN. 13, 1808
MAY 7, 1873
SECRETARY OF THE TREASURY
UNDER PRESIDENT LINCOLN
OHIO'S JUSTICE U.S. SUPREME COURT

THE CHASE HOUSE

A famous banker's birthplace

Born in 1808, Salmon P. Chase spent the first decade of his life in the village of Cornish, New Hampshire. By the age of eleven he was sent to Ohio to live with his uncle, an Episcopal bishop, but in time Chase returned to New Hampshire to attend Dartmouth College. Eventually he was elected to the United States Senate, and after six years was elected to two terms as Ohio's governor, after which he returned to Washington and the Senate. From there, this remarkable American went on to serve Abraham Lincoln as Secretary of the Treasury, and soon thereafter was appointed Chief Justice of the United States, where he served until his death in 1873. In his lifetime he was a tireless anti-slavery spokesman; founded the Republican Party; had his picture engraved on the $10,000 bill; and gave his name to the Chase Manhattan Bank.

Chase's birthplace, one of the finest homes in this tiny Connecticut River valley village, has been meticulously restored as a bed and breakfast inn by Peter Burling, an attorney and a member of Cornish's town planning board. He commissioned the talents of experienced restoration experts, who thoroughly and carefully pieced together the checkered history of the house.

The result is a stunning, early Federal house that sits on the banks of the river, surrounded by stately shade trees. The furnishings throughout are elegant, comfortable, and simple, and they enhance one's enjoyment of the home's lovely architectural detail.

The full breakfast that is served each morning prepares one for exploring the wooded New England countryside. The Chase House is centrally located nearby Hanover and Dartmouth College, as well as the sophisticated shops and restaurants of Woodstock, Vermont.

THE CHASE HOUSE. RR 2, Box 909, Cornish, NH 03745; (603) 675-5391; Hal and Marilyn Wallace, Pete Burling, hosts. Open all year. Six rooms, 4 with private baths, 2 sharing. Rates: $65 to $85, with full breakfast. Children welcome; no pets; Visa/MasterCard accepted. Canoeing, hiking, cross-country skiing on trails on premises. Interesting dining in area.

DIRECTIONS: from I-91 North take Ascutney exit across Connecticut River, turn north on Rte. 12A for 5 miles to inn.

High ceilings make for grand spaces.

CRAB APPLE INN

With an English country garden

Crab Apple Inn is charming—from its well-preserved doorway fan to its babbling brook. White trim and black shutters complement the 1835 brick Federal building and the white picket fence that encloses the tidy house and its brilliantly colored English country garden.

Two cheery third-floor rooms boast the best view, overlooking most of the inn's two-and-a-half acres and Crosby Mountain. Yet every guest gets something special: an arched canopy bed, a hand-carved sleigh bed, a brass bed. Intimate and cozy, the household harbors a warmth that emanates primarily from its two owners, Carolyn and Bill Crenson, who had been planning to open a bed and breakfast for years.

An award-winning sign.

When they moved in, they took over management of the inn. "It was twenty below. Pipes were freezing, snow, wind. And we had guests two days later—a full house," recounts Carolyn.

This is indeed snow country, the gateway to the White Mountains. Polar Caves is one mile down the road, and Waterville Valley and Tenney Mountain, minutes away.

Warm weather enthusiasts can wade in nearby Newfound Lake or relax on the brick patio, sipping iced tea by the French doors, with candy and fresh fruit available. Breakfasts, whether indoors or *al fresco*, feature refreshingly simple, home-cooked country fare.

Carolyn and Bill attend to the small details that make life more enjoyable when on the road—leaving terry cloth robes for those guests in rooms with shared baths and offering wine or tea and snacks in the afternoon.

CRAB APPLE INN, Rte. 25, RFD 2, Box 200B, West Plymouth, NH 03264; (603) 536-4476; Carolyn and Bill Crenson, innkeepers. Open all year. Five guest rooms; suite and one bedroom have private bath; two rooms share one bath. Rates: $60 to $75, including a country breakfast. Children over 8 welcome; no pets. MasterCard/Visa. All-season recreation in area; antiquing. Good restaurants nearby.

DIRECTIONS: from I-93, take exit 26 and head west on Rte. 25. The inn is 4 miles from the interstate on the left.

". . . and the snow lay round about, deep and crisp and even."

HAVERHILL INN

1810 Federal house near village green

n its heyday, Haverhill was a county seat, and rosperity left its mark in the form of grand nansions, many sitting high on the rise overlooking the lovely Connecticut River and Vermont's olling hills. When the railroad bypassed Havrhill, the town stood still. Today you can't find grocery, drug store, or even a general store. Modernization" has never touched this island of eauty, and Haverhill is richer for its loss.

The Haverhill Inn is one of those elegantly roportioned mansions that overlooks the river. emanates a calm and tranquility that speaks ell of its keepers, Katharine DeBoer and Stephen ampbell. But this peaceful atmosphere can also e traced to older inhabitants. Three volumes of ata and letters have been compiled on the history f Haverhill and the house. Tracing its lineage,

readers discover that each owner bestowed genuine love on this home. This fortunate history has left its mark.

Today the inn comprises four guest rooms. Each is spacious and each has a working fireplace. The living room, which contains Katharine's baby grand piano, is a comfortable gathering spot, where guests can enjoy a glass of sherry, cup of tea, or a good read. Both Katharine and Stephen pursue careers outside innkeeping. She is a soloist soprano, who gives concerts and teaches. Stephen has a thriving career as a computer programming consultant. Since most of their work is done out of their home, the inn is always well tended.

In summer Katharine plants a large garden from which guests enjoy a bounty of fresh produce. Stephen is a dedicated and gifted cook who makes breakfast a very special event, especially on Sunday.

HAVERHILL INN, Dartmouth College Hwy., Rte. 10, Haverhill, NH 03765; (603) 989-5961; Stephen Campbell and Katharine DeBoer, hosts. French spoken. 1810 Federal style house on quiet street near village green. Open all year. Four guest rooms, all private baths. Rates: $50 single, $65 double, with $10 per additional occupant, including full breakfast. Afternoon tea and coffee. Restaurants nearby. Older children welcome; pets discouraged; smoking restricted; no credit cards.

DIRECTIONS: from Hanover, take Rte. 10 North 27 miles. From NYC (6 hrs.), take I-91 North to exit 15 (Fairlee, Vt.), cross river to Orford, N.H., and proceed north on Rte. 10. From Boston, I-93 to Plymouth, Rte. 25 west to Haverhill.

AMOS A. PARKER HOUSE

The place to get away from it all

wandering off the beaten track is your idea of ne perfect getaway, the southwest corner of New lampshire beckons. Visitors to the area come to scape the rat race and to get in touch with life's ssentials. The area is richly blessed with sparing lakes, ponds, and streams; groves of rhododendron that burst into bloom each summer; nd maple trees that glow in the autumn and roduce sweet syrup in early spring. The region dominated by Mount Monadnock, which over ne years has inspired such artists as Emerson, ipling, and Kilmer. Thoreau climbed to the mmit three times, and the mountain was a nstant companion during his solitary sojourn Walden Pond.

Such relaxed and gentle surroundings are comemented by the historic Amos A. Parker House.

ne Great Room, so-named because everyone exclaims, Vhat a great room!" when they first see it.

A stay at this colonial bed and breakfast inn is like visiting a favorite relative. Innkeeper Freda Houpt is the inn's genial host and she makes visitors feel a part of this fine old place. The earliest section of the house dates back to the mid-1700s, with an addition built in 1780. Freda has filled her home with comfortable furnishings that match the Federal period, preferring the sturdiness of good eighteenth and nineteenth-century reproductions to the delicacy of fine antiques. She is justifiably proud of her gardens and her lawn, which sweeps gently to an active beaver pond at the edge of the grass.

Besides the natural beauty of the area, visitors enjoy cultural events, such as plays and concerts, offered throughout the year. Also, the village of Fitzwilliam (which, for trivia buffs, is the only town in the United States bearing that name), as well as the surrounding countryside, is well-known for the quality of its antiques and crafts shops.

AMOS A. PARKER HOUSE, Box 202, Rte. 119, Fitzwilliam, NH 03447; (603) 585-6540; Freda B. Houpt, proprietor. Open all year. Five rooms sharing 3 baths. Rates: $50 to $75 with full breakfast. Children over 10 welcome; no pets; no credit cards. Canoeing, golf, tennis, hiking, biking, climbing in area. Country inn dining nearby.

DIRECTIONS: from I-91 take exit 28A to Rte. 10 North to Rte. 119 East. From Boston take Rte. 2 West to Rte. 140 North to Rte. 12 North to Rte. 119 West.

BEAL HOUSE INN

Candlelit breakfasts

Ann and Jim Carver, proprietors of this "living antique shop" bed and breakfast establishment came to this venture with three talented sons; one who restores and upholsters the furniture, one with a degree in hotel management, and one who lends general support and good cheer. In short this is a family operation of grand proportions.

Built in 1833, the Beal House Inn began as a Federal Renaissance farmhouse. Over the years, the house and barn slowly grew together, connecting through the carriage house. The five-stall horse barn became an antiques shop and thus began the tradition for providing travelers with warm New England hospitality and newfound treasures.

Each of the fourteen rooms in this hostelry has its own character—canopied, brass, spool, and four poster beds; hooked and braided rugs; comfortable wing chairs. Everything you look at, sleep atop, sit in, or admire is for sale. What better way to shop for a bed or chair than to live with it for a time. An antiques shop/inn makes for an everchanging setting, since a room that loses its elaborate Victorian canopied bed might in turn gain a weighty sleigh bed or a pair of simple pencil post twins.

Breakfast is a delightful experience in a candlelit dining room where long tables are set with Blue Willow plates on lovely antique red tablecloths. Hot popovers, the inn's specialty, begins the meal, with a large selection of fruit juices, homemade breads, and beverages following. French toast, creamy scrambled eggs served in white glass hens-on-nests, ham, bacon and fresh ground sausage are served à la carte.

The parlor features games, books, stereo views, and a fireplace. And the second floor has an inviting book-nook and a deck that reaches out to the back lawn and the terraced woods.

THE BEAL HOUSE INN, Main St., Littleton, NH 03561; (603) 444-2661; the Carver family, hosts. Frame Federal-style house has been inn-*cum*-antiques-shop for over 50 years. Open all year. Fourteen guest rooms, twelve with private baths. Rates $35 to $120, including suites, according to season and amenities. Continental breakfast included; additional charge for full country breakfast served tavern-style. Evening tea and snacks. Current menus and reservation service for local dining. Children eight and over welcome; pet boarding nearby; smoking restricted; major credit cards.

DIRECTIONS: from I-93, take exit 41 into Littleton. Turn left onto Main St. to inn, at junction of Rtes. 18 and 302.

Left, the staircase leading to the guest rooms is bedecked with whimsical bookends and doorstops.

VERMONT

Wonderful hosts in the back country

Cynthia and Lester Firschein, both anthropologists, have turned the Parmenter House into a backcountry hiker's dream. Hikers themselves, they have made it their business to acquaint themselves with the dirt roads and paths around Belmont, which include trail heads for the Long and Appalachian trails. Cynthia knows of at least ten day-hike segments within half an hour of their house. Opting for a more speedy tour, guests can rent trail bikes at the inn for $25 a day. The rate covers a generous box lunch and being picked up at the end of the day. Cynthia and Lester have made copies of their favorite routes: to an herb farm; along Towner Road (the most photographed road in Vermont); and to a music camp that offers classical concerts.

Guests often take breakfast on the deck out back. Afternoon tea is served in the Eastlake-inspired living room amid paintings and screens by Alfred Rasmussen, Cynthia's grandfather. Her mother carved the walnut dining room set, and her uncles painted the trunk in which her grandmother brought her belongings from Denmark.

The appeal of the Parmenter House, however, lies with its laid-back hosts, who will spontaneously gather a group for a caravan ride and picnic or take guests to visit the Weston Priority, a serenely picturesque Benedictine monastery.

THE PARMENTER HOUSE, P.O. Box 106, Belmont, VT 05730; (802) 259-2009; Cynthia and Lester Firschein, hosts. Spanish and French spoken. Open all year. Five guest rooms, each with private bath. Rates; $65 to $80; additional person, $15. Includes continental breakfast. MasterCard/Visa for deposits only. Theater, many outdoor activities, Ludlow restaurants nearby.

DIRECTIONS: from I-91, take exit 6 and then Rte. 103 through Chester and Ludlow. After Ludlow center and Okemo Access Road (which will be on left), stay on Rte. 103 until you come to a blinking light. Turn left at this light. After two miles you will come to the center of Belmont, marked by a four-cornered intersection. Turn left; the Parmenter House is the second house on your left, directly opposite the white church.

Left, tea in the parlor, amid the Bradbury and Bradbury wallpaper. Above, innkeeper Cynthia Firschein at breakfast.

SOUTH SHIRE INN

Special comfort and personality

Bennington, Vermont is a bustling New England village, tucked securely in a broad and handsome Green Mountain valley. The South Shire Inn, which sits at the edge of the handsome residential district, is perfectly situated between historic Old Bennington, with its famous Battle Monument, Old First Church, and Old Burying Ground (resting place of poet Robert Frost) and the shops and restaurants that cluster at the village center.

The house dates back to the late 1800s, when Bennington's prominent Graves family built a compound of five adjoining mansions to accommodate the burgeoning clan. No expense was spared when they raised Louis Graves' Queen Anne Victorian home, and today this solid and spacious mansion serves as contemporary Bennington's finest bed and breakfast inn.

Owned and operated by Mark and Suzanne Gashi, the South Shire Inn is striking and handsome. Of special note on the first floor is the very grand library, paneled with lustrous Honduran mahogany and outfitted with a working, tile-faced fireplace and built-in, leaded glass bookcases. The adjoining breakfast room is so encrusted with rococo plaster friezes it could put a wedding cake to shame.

One bedroom is found on the inn's first floor and the remainder are located upstairs, on the second and third floors. Each has its own special comfort and personality. Several spacious chambers come complete with working fireplaces, and Suzanne and Mark thoughtfully gave their smallest room a beautifully designed tiled bathroom, ample enough for a visiting dignitary.

The Gashis proceed with great care and thought when it comes to restoring and furnishing the inn, which adds to the sense of solidity and "rightness" about the place. Currently, plans are in the works to convert the handsomely appointed carriage house, located just behind the inn, into luxurious guest suites.

THE SOUTH SHIRE INN, 124 Elm Street, Bennington, VT 05201; (802) 447-3839; Mark and Suzanne Gashi, hosts. Open all year. Five rooms with private baths. Rates: $60 to $105, varying seasonally. Children over 14 welcome; no pets; Visa/MasterCard/American Express. Fishing, golf, hiking, antiquing, museums, outlet stores in area. Many restaurants for dining.

DIRECTIONS: take Elm St. off Rte. 7 between Jefferson and Dewey.

Left and above, the elegant atmosphere of the second-floor guest rooms.

SHOREHAM INN AND COUNTRY STORE

A tiny town on Lake Champlain

Surrounded by apple orchards and dairy farms, and bordered on one side by Lake Champlain's sinuous tail, the Shoreham Inn and its adjoining Country Store form the heart of tiny Shoreham, Vermont. The inn's atmosphere, reflecting its beautiful setting and kind proprietors, is warm, gentle, and welcoming.

Built in 1799 as a public house, it allows today's inngoers to walk the same wooden floorboards that its first visitors trod. These wide planks are partially hidden by lustrous old area rugs and an irregular collection of antiques— none matches, but all work together—that please the eye and comfort the spirit.

Cleo and Fred Alter love original art, a taste fully developed during the days they worked together in printing and graphic design, and they exercise this love by showing the work of gifted local artists. Not a gallery per se, the inn doesn't sell work but the Alters do take pleasure in sharing beautiful things with others.

Breakfast is low-keyed. On each table guests find a canning jar filled with granola, pitchers of milk and juice, local honey and preserves, muffins or scones, and cheese. Since this is apple country, Cleo always serves the fruit in one form or another. Glass cookie jars in the center of each large dining table are always stocked with homebaked sweets for snackers.

The Country Store, just next to the inn, supplies everything from magazines and groceries to hardware and wine. The Alters operate a small delicatessen in back, where you can order a pizza or sandwiches and salads. Picnic tables on the village green beckon on a summer day.

SHOREHAM INN AND COUNTRY STORE, Shoreham, VT 05770; (802) 897-5081; Cleo and Fred Alter, hosts. Built as an inn in 1799, the Shoreham served as a way station for floating railroad bridge and ferry across Lake Champlain. Open all year. Eleven guest rooms, some accommodating four people, shared baths. Rates $35 single, $65 double, including country breakfast. Numerous restaurants in area. Children welcome; no pets; no credit cards. Area offers aquatic and other sports, museums, Ft. Ticonderoga, Morgan horse farm.

DIRECTIONS: inn is 12 miles southwest of Middlebury. Follow Rte. 22A from Fairhaven to Rte. 74 west. From Burlington, take 7 south to 22A at Vergennes, then take 74 west into Shoreham. Ticonderoga ferry operates to and from Shoreham.

MAPLE CREST FARM

Ancestral home and working dairy farm

Maple Crest Farm has been in the same family for five generations, ever since it opened its doors as Gleason Tavern in 1808. The resulting atmosphere is multi-layered and rich. This is not a manicured vacation resort; rather it is a working dairy farm with a hundred head of cattle.

The architectural styles in the farmhouse are interesting. Gleason built a colonial structure with Federal embellishments. Enter the Victorian age with its mandatory decorative porches and ornate hearth treatments. And finally the twentieth century brought with it inelegant linoleum and acoustical tiles. Though each age will still be represented, Donna Smith, Maple Crest's gracious hostess, is slowly but surely removing the more offensive "improvements" and uncovering original floors and beams.

Guests spend hours poring over diaries and the family bible, observing a dairy farm at work, and in the spring participating in maple-sugaring.

The dairy barns.

Acres of hiking paths become excellent cross-country ski trails when snow cooperates. All in all, Maple Crest Farm is a diamond in the rough and well worth a visit.

MAPLE CREST FARM , Box 120, Cuttingsville, VT 05738; (802) 492-3367; William and Donna Smith, hosts. Closed first two weeks of November, Thanksgiving, Christmas Eve and Day. Four guest rooms with shared bath, one two-bedroom apartment. Rates $40 to $50 double; full breakfast included. Restaurants in nearby Rutland. Children over 6; no pets; smoking permitted; no credit cards.

DIRECTIONS: from Manchester, take Rte. 7 north to Rte. 103 (just south of Rutland). Turn right on 103, cross railroad tracks, and drive up the hill. Watch for "Meadow Sweet Herb Farm" sign. At hilltop, bear left on Lincoln Hill Rd. and continue 2 miles; farm is in Shrewesbury on right, across from church and meeting hall.

Donna's breakfast bread.

MAPLEWOOD INN

A classic farmhouse in western Vermont

The emerald hills of western Vermont are dappled with lush farm fields, picturesque orchards, and crystal lakes. The Maplewood Inn is nestled in the heart of this natural paradise, making it the perfect home base for exploring the area.

The inn is a classic New England farmhouse— its clapboards painted sparkling white with colonial red doors and shutters. The Greek Revival "core" of the house was built around 1850; from 1880 to 1979 the farm produced enough milk to make Maplewood Farm the area's most prominent dairy. Old-fashioned milk bottles and artifacts from the dairy have been unearthed and gathered together by innkeepers Cindy and Paul Soder, and this nostalgic collection is on display in

several cupboards in the first-floor common rooms. A long, pillared wing, which predates the Greek Revival portion of the house, provides shelter for an inviting porch, whose western aspect pleases sunset aficionados.

The Soders welcome guests to their spotlessly-maintained inn through the breakfast room, where each morning an "expanded" continental breakfast—including fresh baked breads, fresh fruit, yogurts, granola or cereals, and hot beverages— is served. The décor of the inn conforms to a fresh country motif: soft colors, and informal antique and reproduction furnishings in a compatible blend of styles and periods. Each bedroom is fresh and comfortable. Two second-floor suites are particularly spacious, each having a private sitting room, and the only guest room on the main floor has its own entrance.

MAPLEWOOD INN, Rte. 22A South, RR1 Box 4460, Fair Haven, VT 05743; (802) 265-8039; Cindy and Paul Soder, hosts. Open all year. Three rooms with private and shared baths and 2 suites with private baths. Rates: $60 to $95 with continental-plus breakfast. Children over 6 with prior approval; no pets; Visa/MasterCard accepted. Croquet and lawn games on premises and water skiing, boating, fishing, hiking, riding, and golfing nearby. Country inn dining in nearby inns.

DIRECTIONS: from Vermont Rte. 4 take Rte. 22A South through Fair Haven for 1 mile. Inn is on the left.

A former dairy farm, from which an old-fashioned milk bottle is shown on page 1.

Impeccable detailing throughout includes this tea cup collection.

THE JACKSON HOUSE AT WOODSTOCK

Elegant décor

The Jackson House at Woodstock is as friendly as it is elegant. Jack Foster greets you warmly upon arrival, offering a pair of "scuffies" as he welcomes you to the house. These comfortable slippers—and the heat lamps in the bathrooms—typify the thought that went into the formation of this bed and breakfast.

With professional flair, Jack decorated the nine guest rooms, imbuing them with a clever sense of style. This is most apparent in the Gloria Swanson Room, a yellow room with primitive maple furniture, maple floor, even a maple picture frame. A photograph of the famous actress graces the dresser. Each room is quite lovely and unique. The Wentworth has a pre-Columbian feel; Cranberry, an oriental mien. The Mary T. Lincoln is a more traditional room in walnut, while the Thornbirds appeals to ocean lovers who delight in the sea green hues and bamboo appointments.

Guests wander down to breakfast from 7:30 to 9:30, sharing conversation around a Jacobean gate-leg table that came from an English pub.

Jack prides himself on the food he serves. A standard morning entrée might be Spinach and Eggs Grisanti, a fragrant egg dish that includes spinach, garlic, and parmesan cheese, or cheese blintzes. Homemade muffins and coffeecake and the normal complement of fruit, juices, jams complete the meal.

THE JACKSON HOUSE AT WOODSTOCK, Rte. 4 West, Woodstock, VT 05091; (802) 457-2065; Jack D. Foster, host. Closed April 1 to May 15 and November 1 to December 15. Nine guest rooms, seven with private baths. Rates: $100 double. Children over 14 welcome; no pets; no smoking. Visa/MasterCard/American Express. Robert Trent Jones golf course, tennis in area. French touring bikes available.

DIRECTIONS: The Jackson House is 1½ miles west of Woodstock Village on Rte. 4

SHIRE INN

Where guests come to relax

One hour from Burlington and halfway between Boston and Montreal, the Shire Inn affords comfort and elegant surroundings for guests traveling through central Vermont.

Love at first sight was the reason the Papas bought the inn. Enclosed by a white picket fence, the house is constructed of handsome Vermont brick with a granite arch curving gracefully over its front door. Spring and summer gardens add color and fragrance; a wooden bridge stands behind the inn and the White River flows past it.

Six distinct guest rooms, all named for counties in Vermont, are furnished with period antiques. Four of them have working fireplaces. All of the bedsteads are dressed with country bedspreads and ample comforters and a generous supply of books and magazines is provided in all rooms.

Breakfast consists of three courses. Favorite entrées include a cream cheese omelet topped with mint, every manner of pancake, including the house specialty, an Eierkuchen spread with an apricot sauce, and baked fruit. Dinners are served during the week by reservation. A minimum two-night weekend includes one six-course dinner which might feature pork chops with caraway stuffing, fillet of sole in wine, chicken in a spice or curry sauce, or swordfish with lime mayonnaise.

Cross-country skiing in Chelsea, downhill skiing in Barnard, swimming and boating on Lake Fairlee, theater, art galleries, and restaurants in nearby Woodstock and Montpelier make the Shire an inn for all seasons.

THE SHIRE INN, P.O. Box 37, Main St., Chelsea, VT 05038; (802) 685-3031; James and Mary Lee Papa, innkeepers. Open all year. Federal-style brick house built in 1832. Six guest rooms, all with private baths, four with working fireplaces. Rates: $65 to $95 double depending upon season. Delicious full breakfast included. Dinner available by advance reservation. Minimum two night weekend including one dinner. Children over 6 welcome; no pets; no smoking; Visa/MasterCard. Cross-country skiing, hiking, antiquing.

DIRECTIONS: from I-89 take the Sharon exit (exit 2) to Rte. 14 to S. Royalton, to Rte. 110 north to Chelsea. From I-91, take the Thetford exit (exit 14) to Rte. 113 north to Chelsea. The inn is on the village's main road, on the left.

Marlboro is the classic New England village, consisting of a church, a post office, and an inn.

WHETSTONE INN

"The nicest inn in New England"

Jean and Harry Boardman moved to southern Vermont from southern California where Harry was secretary general for the Council for Biology and Human Affairs at the Salk Institute and where Jean edited a linguistics journal. Over the years Harry had stayed at this historic inn while in the area to give seminars on humanist subjects. And though neither he nor Jean had ever given thought to becoming innkeepers, six months after discovering that this 1786 tavern was for sale, the Boardmans were running the Whetstone Inn.

Warmhearted, intellectually stimulating, and decorated in a no-frills, comfortable style, the Whetstone elicits spontaneous testimonials. Rosy-cheeked from an afternoon of cross-country skiing, one thoroughly satisfied guest burst forth with unrestrained enthusiasm: "Do you want to know about this place? It's the epitome, the absolutely nicest inn in New England. Harry and Jean make it what it is. Jean is just the best chef. You can't believe what her cooking is like. . ."

Jean's cooking is, indeed, renowned, from her masterful handling of breakfast foods to the dinners she creates several times a week. Fortunate patrons might dine on homemade soup; leg of lamb with plum sauce; filet of beef or veal with white wine sauce; fresh salad; and, for dessert, a pie shell filled with chocolate mousse, or, the all-time favorite, apple cheddar cheese pie.

Tiny Marlboro is a classic, picture postcard village as well as a year-round resort. Summer brings many joys including the seven-week Marlboro Music Festival, a feast of chamber music with Rudolph Serkin as artistic director. Luminaries from the world of music, from Avery Fisher to Jean Pierre Rampal, might be table partners at one of Jean's dinners. Fall color is brilliant, and the loveliness of the flowers and vivid greens of spring beggars description. During the winter season the Whetstone offers excellent cross-country skiing on its eleven acres of hills and meadows, while downhill skiing is found a short drive away.

A "pre-Murphy" bed.

Left, heading for the cross-country ski trails.

WHETSTONE INN, Marlboro, VT 05344; (802) 254-2500; Jean and Harry Boardman, Hosts. French and some German spoken. Post-and-beam construction inn, built as a tavern around 1786. Open year-round. Eleven guest rooms, some with kitchenettes, some that accommodate four; shared and private baths. Rates: $25 singles, $55 to $70 doubles; $2 infant, $6 child, $10 third adult (15 and above). Hearty breakfast served; variety of good restaurants in area. Pets accepted; smoking discouraged; checks accepted; Downhill and cross-country skiing, hiking.

DIRECTIONS: drive 8 miles west from Brattleboro, Vt., on Rte. 9. Marlboro is ¼ mile off Rte. 9.

1811 HOUSE

A classic inn; a classic village

This is not just another inn. The groomed and elegant 1811 House is impeccable inside and out. When Mary and Jack Hirst found this historic building, ideally situated next to the classic New England spired church on the equally classic Manchester village green, it was in need of complete renovation. They began by removing aluminum siding that encased the structure and hiring eight men to remove two centuries of paint. It took workers ten full weeks to uncover the original wood. Then the Federal capitals and moldings began to fall apart. So the Hirsts copied all of the embellishments and reinstated identical decorative moldings. Finally, the "two-over-two" Victorian cylinder glass windows were replaced by colonial-style twelve-pane glass. Jack didn't rest until each pane was filled with irregular antique glass.

The Hirsts tackled the interior with the same dedication and energy, painstakingly restoring original detail and adding private baths for each

A second floor guest room.

of the ten bedrooms. In the center of the building they created an English pub, in honor of Mary's homeland, complete with dartboard and working fireplace.

All of the rooms in the house are simple and lovely. The first-floor parlors and dining room are furnished from Mary's collection of fine English antiques, crystal, and paintings of country scenes. Each bedroom has its own color scheme and personality.

Britain inspires American inns, and Mary's authentic English breakfast shows us one reason why. Guests might be treated to kippers, sautéed chicken livers, or sole meunière; grilled tomatoes; sautéed apples and mushrooms, in addition to eggs, bacon, fried bread, and fresh-squeezed orange juice, all served on fine china and crystal.

1811 HOUSE, Manchester Village, VT 05254; (802) 362-1811; Mary and Jack Hirst, Pat and Jeremy David, hosts. Excellent example of Federal architecture, which was long a famous summer resort in the 1800s. Open year-round. Fourteen guest rooms, private baths. Rates: $100 to $150 double. Full English-style breakfast. No children under sixteen; no pets; major credit cards. Excellent dining in the area and occasional dinners served on premises for guests. Hiking, fishing, tennis, golf, swimming, antiquing, winter skiing.

DIRECTIONS: from Bennington, Vt., drive north on historic Rte. 7A. Inn is in Manchester Village on the green, next to the Congregational Church (with spire).

BEAUCHAMP PLACE

Anglophiles with exquisite taste

Roy and Georgia Beauchamp lived in England for fifteen years before they retired to the sophisticated, tidy village of Brandon. In planning, this astonishingly beautiful inn, they decided to adopt the amenities of Europe, adding touches characteristic of America's unique style of relaxation. In keeping with the style of this mansard-roofed manor house, Georgia chose wallpaper from the Victorian Historical Society Book and ordered new embossed tin ceilings for the third floor. Each of the eight bedrooms is furnished with Victorian and Empire pieces, many of which came from former Vermont estates. Down duvets, individually controlled heat, and plush, color-coordinated towels afford individual comfort.

A veritable museum collection of furniture and decorative art dwells in the downstairs common rooms: a burled walnut sideboard that survived the bombing in World War II, a 1765 Branson, Hull grandfather moon clock, Battersea Halcyon Days enamel boxes, a Royal Crown Darby collection, and soft, pink Venetian glass from Murano to name a few.

Anglophiles at heart, the Beauchamps became increasingly interested in genealogy when they lived abroad. Georgia researched church records in Britain, tracing her ancestors, who include two of the original Jamestown settlers, a poet laureate buried in Westminster Abbey and a dissenter buried in the Tower of London. Roy's lineage is equally impressive. His family came from Normandy with William the Conqueror in 1066. A recent relative was the keeper of the seal of Maryland, and first secretary of that state, in 1665.

BEAUCHAMP PLACE, Rte. 7, 31 Franklin Street, Brandon, VT 05733; (802) 247-3905; Roy and Georgia Beauchamp, innkeepers. Open all year. Eight rooms share four baths. Rates: $70 to $85; includes full breakfast with freshly baked goods. Not suggested for children under sixteen; no pets; no smoking; American Express/MasterCard/Visa. Golf, tennis, skiing, watersports, croquet, sleigh rides; antiquing. Near to Middlebury College.

DIRECTIONS: from Rte. 4, turn onto Rte. 7 heading north. Brandon sits at the junction of Rte. 7 and 73. The inn is located on the right, just past the center of town, on Rte. 7.

The wood paneled staircase, laden with teddy bears.

HUGGING BEAR INN

he healing power of Teddy Bears

he warm spirit of the Hugging Bear embraces ne and all who pass through its doors. Paul and Georgette Thomas came to innkeeping from caring areers, Georgette as a counselor with a degree n social work, and Paul as an attorney and dedicated human-rights advocate. When they discovered an article in *Prevention* magazine outing the healing power of teddy bears, they new they had found the perfect theme for this ambling, Queen Anne Victorian bed and breakast inn, which sits on the main street of historic Chester, Vermont.

Teddy bears are found in every nook and cranny f the inn. They play the piano, peek out from potted plants, climb the lovely Victorian staircase, nd perch atop each bed. Besides the inn, the Hugging Bear Shoppe, located in the basement, is dedicated to the irresistible charms of the teddy bear.

Because the Thomases are sensitive to the difficulties of parents traveling with children, they welcome families with open arms. Children are encouraged to choose the teddy bears of their choice to sleep with at night, and occasionally they may borrow favorites from the shop, as long as they promise to return them "to work" by 8 A.M. But it isn't strictly children who are moved by this colorful menagerie of huggable creatures. The Thomases report that a majority of adults who pass through their inn fall under the spell of teddy bear power.

THE HUGGING BEAR INN & SHOPPE, Main Street, Box 32, Chester, VT 05143; (802) 875-2412; Georgette, Paul, and Diane Thomas, hosts. Open all year. Six rooms with private baths. Rates: $70 to $75 per room, with full breakfast and afternoon cheese, crackers, and cider. Children welcome; pets limited; no smoking; Visa/MasterCard accepted. Four-room bear shop. Hugging teddy bears encouraged. Badminton, volleyball, croquet on premises. Antiquing, flea markets, auctions, biking, golf, tennis nearby. A special event occurs on the second weekend of December, when the town celebrates a Victorian Christmas.. Lighting trees, caroling, and wearing Victorian costumes are among the colorful activities. The inn provides period costumes for guests to wear to a reception for Santa Claus, who arrives in a horse drawn carriage or sled, snow permitting.

DIRECTIONS: located on the main street of Chester, Vermont.

MASSACHUSETTS

NORTHFIELD COUNTRY HOUSE

A well-kept secret revealed

Hidden in the hills of the beautiful Connecticut River Valley, Northfield Country House is one of those special places that visitors hope to keep a secret, all to themselves.

The aura of romance begins as you wind your way up the drive. Trees suddenly part to reveal a gracefully proportioned English manor house built in 1901 by a wealthy Boston shipbuilder who had an eye for beauty and the purse to pursue it. He insisted upon the finest handcarved cherry wainscoting, mantels, and doors; a broad staircase; leaded glass windows; and a twelve-foot stone hearth in which is embedded the message, "Love Warms The Heart As Fire The Hearth."

Andrea Dale's country house has been decorated with an eye to combining design and color into an art form. The living room with its stone hearth and three plush and generous couches invites quiet relaxation and easy conversation.

The house offers the comforts of home plus special extras—pretty sitting areas in all of the guest rooms, rich Bokara and Herziz carpets to cushion the foot. A romantic hideaway with working fireplace, velvet settee, and thick comforter on an antique bed feels rich and warm; another blue and white chamber complete with brass and iron bedstead and white wicker armchair is crisp, fresh, and old-fashioned.

Breakfast, which is served on the porch in the summer and in the cherry-paneled dining room when the weather is wet or cold, is simply splendid, with popovers and cheese and mushroom omelets the popular fare. *Prix fixe* dinners are offered several times a week.

NORTHFIELD COUNTRY HOUSE, School St., Northfield, MA 01360; (413) 498-2692; Andrea Dale, owner. English manor house set on 16 acres. Open year-round. Seven guest rooms, shared baths. Rates: $40 to $70. Full breakfast served daily. Children 10 and over; no pets; Visa/MasterCard; checks accepted.

DIRECTIONS: take I-91 to Exit 28A. Follow Rte. 10 north to Northfield Center. School St. is in center of town, at the firehouse. Turn at firehouse and drive 9/10 of a mile. Inn driveway is on right. *Note:* Since street becomes narrow dirt road, driving in snowy or wet conditions can be difficult. Please have good tires!

THE OLD INN ON THE GREEN

A sleepy village floodlit at night

Brad Wagstaff bought this charming eighteenth-century inn as a restoration project a half-dozen years ago. Leslie Miller came to the Berkshires to train as a baker, rented a room in the partially renovated inn, and fell in love with Brad and the Berkshires.

The New Marlborough green is pastoral and idyllic, a sleepy village whose cluster of Greek Revival relics—most especially the Town Meeting House, dramatically floodlit at night—reflects a burst of commerce long since past. A short walk along the town's quiet main road takes strollers past Brad's flock of sheep and large herd of dairy cattle. Wander down the lane just next to the inn to discover some of the most spectacular scenery in the Berkshire Mountains.

The inn, which is being meticulously restored to its original glory, is casual and wonderfully atmospheric. Bedrooms are furnished with a combination of classic antiques and funky art deco and forties accoutrements. The second-floor balcony was made for a leisurely morning of reading, coffee drinking, or just watching the sun move higher in the sky.

The inn features a formal dinner each Friday and Saturday night, served in the four downstairs dining rooms. With the aid of a talented local chef, Leslie and Brad offer a five-course *prix fixe* menu that changes with the seasons and unfolds beautifully in the soft glow of candlelight and firelight.

THE OLD INN ON THE GREEN, New Marlborough, MA 01230; (413) 229-7924; Leslie Miller and Brad Wagstaff, hosts. Spanish spoken by Leslie. Built in 1760 as an inn, this Greek Revival gem also once served as tavern, stagecoach stop, general store, and post office. Open year-round. Five guest rooms; private and shared baths. Rates: $75 to $110 per room. Continental breakfast. No pets; checks accepted; no credit cards. Summer theater nearby; excellent dining in area.

DIRECTIONS: from New York City, take Taconic Pkwy. to Rte. 23 exit. Take 23 through Great Barrington and go east toward Monterrey. Turn right on Rte. 57 before Monterry and follow for 5.7 miles. From Boston, take Mass. Tnpke. to Lee exit. Take Rte. 7 through Stockbridge to Rte. 23, and 23 toward Monterrey following directions above.

CORNELL HOUSE

Cabaret conviviality still echoes here

New owners Jack and Vicki D'Elia have completely renovated the stately Cornell House. A speakeasy during Prohibition, this graceful Queen Anne Victorian still echoes its colorful past.

Facing the four-hundred-acre Kennedy Park, open to the public year-round, the communal breakfast parlor with floor-to-ceiling windows is a favorite gathering spot. A deck with tables and colorful umbrellas can be glimpsed from the dining table, and guests are welcome to eat breakfast al fresco, when the weather permits. In the evening, dining tables transform into game tables and conversation often continues into the wee hours.

Behind the main house is Hill House, a two-story converted barn, especially charming in warm months when shuttered windows are accented with flowering window boxes. Newly developed into four luxury apartments, each unit has its own bedroom, living room, and dining room and features a private deck, galley kitchen, Jacuzzi, fireplace, and air conditioning.

Here, in a location central to both busy Lenox Center and Tanglewood, the D'Elias go all out for their guests, making reservations, supplying schedules, providing knowing suggestions, finding hiking trails, helping them on their way, and, finally, welcoming them back home with an inexhaustable supply of wine and cheese.

CORNELL HOUSE. 197 Pittsfield Rd., Lenox, MA 01240; (413) 637-0562; Jack and Vicki D'Elia, hosts. Charming inn, circa 1888, Victorian-style. Open year-round. Nine guest rooms in main house, four luxury suites in "Hill House," all with private baths. Three night minimum in season. Rates: $330 to $375 for two people for three nights, $65 to $75 per night during week, $895 per week for suite. Off-season specials. Rates include light breakfast; excellent dining nearby. No children in main house; no pets; Visa/MasterCard. The Berkshires offer year-round recreation, cultural events, historic events, antiques.

DIRECTIONS: from New York City, take the Taconic Pkwy. to Rte. 23 exit. Take 23E through Great Barrington to Rte. 7. Take Rte. 7 to Rte. 7A (Lenox Centre) and turn left. Drive through Lenox and up hill to inn on left, just past church. From Mass. Turnpike, take Lee exit 2. Turn right onto Rte. 20W and drive through Lee. Turn left onto Rte. 183 and proceed to Lenox Centre.

BULLFROG BED & BREAKFAST

For weary travelers

In the heart of Mohawk Trail and sugar maple country, adventurous visitors will find the Bullfrog Bed and Breakfast. Lucille Thibault converted her children's rooms into plain, uncluttered nooks for weary travelers. Instead of age-old antiques and cunningly designed handcrafts, she emphasizes true hospitality and good country cooking. And the raspberries, gooseberries, and blueberries she grows make an appearance at most of her country-style breakfasts.

Breakfast around the long table is a lush affair in any season because Lucille's nurtured houseplants hang at every level along the multi-paned windowed wall. Summer guests can hear the chorus of frogs in the pond out back and might even catch a glimpse of the gray horse trotting behind the house.

If you arrive in late winter or early spring as the thaw sets in, her son David may be out sugaring, boiling down the sap collected from their "sugar orchard" next door.

BULLFROG BED AND BREAKFAST, Box 210, Star Route, Ashfield, MA 01330; (413) 628-4493; Lucille Thibault, host. Open year-round. French spoken. Five guest rooms with private and shared baths. Rates: $40, single; $50 to $65, double; includes hearty breakfast. Children welcome; no pets; no smoking preferred; no credit cards. Spring-fed pond has good swimming; Mohawk Trail; Old Deerfield museums; Hoosac Tunnel Museum; antiquing.

DIRECTIONS: from Rte. 91, take exit 24 (S. Deerfield) to 116W through Conway. Begin watching for green mile markers. At approximately mile 42½, the farmhouse is on the right (by Murray Rd.)

Breakfast is cooked on this wood stove.

MERRELL TAVERN INN

Fine antiques in a stagecoach inn

Catering to travelers since the 1800s, the Merrell Tavern has been painstakingly resto to its former glory by Charles and Faith Reynol It is now elegantly furnished with fine Shera and Heppelwhite antiques the Reynolds h collected over twenty-five years. Canopied, fo poster, and pencil-post bedsteads with del mattresses, sought out for their exquisite comf ensure a pleasurable night's sleep. In the morn guests gather in the tavern for breakfast, wh may feature Charles' special omelets, pancak and sausages, or perhaps a new find fron cookbook. A visit will reveal more treasures; th is not space here to do them justice.

MERRELL TAVERN INN, Rte. 102, South Lee., MA 01260; (4 243-1794; Charles and Faith Reynolds, hosts. Closed Christ Eve and Day. Eight guest rooms, three with fireplaces, all v private baths. Rates: $55 to $120 double, according to sea and amenities, weekend packages available. All rates incl full breakfast. No pets; major credit cards.

DIRECTIONS: exit Mass. Turnpike at Lee (exit 2) and fo Rte. 102 three miles toward Stockbridge.

HAUS ANDREAS

Bed and breakfast with amenities

Haus Andreas, a full-service bed and breakfast, is a vacation in itself where hospitality and entertainment are the focus. Overlooking a pastoral view, the colonial mansion was built by a soldier of the American Revolution. During the summer of 1942, the estate became the residence of Queen Wilhelmina of the Netherlands and members of the royal family.

Continental breakfast at the house is elegant, with white linen, china, silver, and a view that is truly inspiring—manicured lawns, birch trees, the orchards, and the mountains.

The formal, well-appointed bedrooms are clean and spare, with fussiness and embellishments kept to a minimum. Antiques in such a setting assume center spotlight.

Outdoors, volleyball, tennis, croquet, and badminton keep many guests busy on the property. The nine-hole golf course across the street attracts many visitors, and bicycles (including a tandem) are available to guests who want to stray a little farther.

Host Gerhard Schmid, an internationally acclaimed chef who has cooked for President Kennedy, the Queen of England, and the Shah of Iran, and his wife Lilliane, the innkeeper at Haus Andreas, also own and operate the Gateways Inn, a sister lodging in nearby Lenox.

HAUS ANDREAS, RR 1, Box 605-B, Stockbridge Road, Lee, MA 01238; (413) 243-3298; Lilliane Schmid, inn-keeper. Nine guest rooms, five with private baths, three with fireplaces; suite available; guesthouse. Rates: weekends in summer range from $80 to $175; midweek, $50 to $100; additional person is approximately $25. A 5% charge is added to the bill for the maids. No pets; no children under ten. No out-of-state checks; Visa/MasterCard. Fine dining throughout the area.

DIRECTIONS: call for specific directions.

Breakfast is served in the main living room.

THE TURNING POINT

Once frequented by Daniel Webster

The acquisition of an old stagecoach stop was a turning point for Shirley and Irv Yost. Situated at the turning point in the road, the inn reflects their commitment to a new lifestyle that includes a growing passion for good food.

Breakfast is worth the trip in itself. As Shirley explains, "During college our children changed to vegetarian diets, and this sparked our interest. After several years of experimenting with this diet, one thing led to another, and before we knew it we opened a bed and breakfast devoted to good, delicious food. A friend of ours has suggested that we bill ourselves as *Breakfast and Bed.*"

The focus of each breakfast is whole grains, though the Yosts can cater to wheat-free and other special diets. An average meal might include feather-light whole wheat-and-bran pancakes served with maple syrup, hot baked fruits or fresh fruit salad, eggs, juice, and grain coffee, herbal tea, and the more common brews. Irv often makes a frittata flavored with a mixture of summer vegetables, a robust concoction that he has earlier frozen to provide a cure for the winter blahs. To fill out each abundant meal, Shirley bakes whole grain fruit breads, which she serves with apple butter or natural peanut butter. The Yosts make every effort to offer foods that contain no preservatives or chemicals.

A stay at the Turning Point, which is furnished with an eclectic mix of antiques and well-loved pieces from their home, is casual, comfortable and very satisfying.

THE TURNING POINT, Rte. 23 and Lake Buel Rd., RD-2 Box 140, Great Barrington, MA 01230; (413) 528-4777; Irv and Shirley Yost, hosts. Federal style older section of house was once tavern-inn frequented by Daniel Webster. Open all year with occasional off-season closings. Seven guest rooms, most sharing baths. Two bedroom cottage. Rates: $45 to $50 single; $70 to $95 double; cottage $165 to $185. Includes elaborate vegetarian breakfast; special diets accommodated. Afternoon tea. Wide range of good dining nearby. Children welcome; no pets; no smoking; no credit cards. Prime Berkshire location offers year-round recreation, sight-seeing, antiquing.

DIRECTIONS: from NYC, take Taconic Pkwy. to Rte. 23. Inn is 21 miles east on Rte. 23 (through Great Barrington) at Lake Buel Rd. From Boston, take Mass. Turnpike to Lee exit (2) onto Rte. 102 W, through Stockbridge to Rte. 750. Follow to Rte. 23, turn left; 2½ miles to inn.

Hostess Marilyn Mudry makes all the quilts.

HAWTHORNE INN

Steeped in American history

Concord, Massachusetts, is among those rare geographical points that seem to emit a force that attracts, inspires, and provokes man to action. The "shot heard round the world" sounded at Old North Bridge and triggered the Revolutionary War. Nearby Walden Pond moved Henry David Thoreau to record profound observations on nature and mankind. Nathaniel Hawthorne, Ralph Waldo Emerson, and the Alcotts made their homes in Concord, nurtured by its ineffable energy.

The Hawthorne Inn offers guests the opportunity to discover Concord and perhaps to experience the force that so inspired America's Transcendentalists. Originally owned by Hawthorne himself, the property has a fascinating history. Good friend Bronson Alcott constructed a Bath House on the land just behind the inn and, using "sylvan architecture," created other elaborate structures made from forest finds. The Bath House was to

be his grandest building, the magnetic point of all his other artworks. Though the building no longer stands, trees planted by these famous neighbors bear silent testimony to its earlier presence. Across from the inn sits Hawthorne's home "Wayside." Grapevine Cottage, where the Concord grape was developed, is another close neighbor.

In the mid-1970s artist Gregory Burch was attracted to Concord and to this house, which was large enough to contain his painting and sculpture studio as well as rooms for wayfarers. He and his wife Marilyn offer guests the comforts of an impeccably maintained and antiques-filled home. Gregory's soapstone bas-relief carvings and energetic paintings, and Marilyn's beautifully designed quilts contribute, along with books of poetry and art, and Mayan and Inca artifacts, to make the Hawthorne Inn a very stimulating haven.

HAWTHORNE INN, 462 Lexington Rd., Concord MA 01742; (617) 369-5610, Gregory Burch and Marilyn Mudry, hosts. Charming inn on site steeped in American history. Open all year. Seven guest rooms, all with private baths. Rates: $85 single, $110 to $150 double, $20 third person. Continental breakfast. No credit cards; no pets. Wide variety of restaurants within 10-minute drive. Equally wide variety of sports and spots of interest in this scenic country.

DIRECTIONS: from Rte. 128–95, take Exit 30-B west for 3½ miles. Bear right at the single blinking light. Inn is one mile on left, across from "Wayside" (Hawthorne and Alcott home).

Elegance on Beacon Hill.

BOSTON—BEACON HILL

PHOTOGRAPHS BY STEVE TOURLENTES

Near Boston Common

Just two blocks from Boston Common, this 1842 brick Federal style townhouse reposes in Beacon Hill, Boston's most desirable neighborhood. Beautiful linden trees line the street. Interesting shops, art galleries, and a pleasing variety of restaurants are all within walking distance.

The hostess, who has filled the rooms with collectibles from more than ninety countries, has traveled extensively throughout the world. Small sculptures, local handicrafts, both primitive and sophisticated, and artworks of every form and kind are on display here. Eighteenth-century European furnishings provide a perfect background for the collection.

Breakfast here is usually made with blueberries—blueberry waffles, blueberry pancakes, or blueberry muffins.

BEACON HILL. 1842 Brick Federal style townhouse. Two guest rooms with shared bath. Central air conditioning. Rates: $60 to $75. Full breakfast upon request. Inquire about children and pets; smoking permitted. Two blocks from Boston Common. *Represented by Bed and Breakfast Associates, Bay Colony Ltd., Boston, MA.*

PHOTOGRAPHS BY STEVE TOURLENTES

BOSTON—BAY VILLAGE

Very near Copley Square

Adjacent to the theater district, this historic 1836 Federal style townhouse is situated in Boston's Bay Village neighborhood. Newly restored, all three guest rooms have been decorated with a mix of country and urban colonial pieces and family heirlooms that will satisfy the most discriminating taste. Hanging on the walls are family portraits that go back three generations. Each room has a working fireplace that does more than its share to add a bit of cheer to a chilly night or inclement morning.

A generous continental breakfast is served. After exchanging morning pleasantries, a visit to the nearby public gardens and Copley Square shops is definitely in order.

BOSTON—CHARLESTON

A unique little stone house

cated on the Freedom Trail, this 1799 Boston ndmark has recently been lovingly restored to original charm. Guests here will long recall ir stay in this unique little stone house.

The hostess, an artist whose body of work ludes a mural on Beacon Hill, has carefully nded period pieces and imaginative color to ate attractive and comfortable surroundings.

A full breakfast is served up for guests, inding hot fresh breads and a variety of teas. e minutes away by public transportation, down- n Boston awaits the visitor with a full range ultural activities, smashing shops and exciting aurants.

RLESTOWN. 1799 Boston landmark. Two guest rooms sharing (Please note that there are steep stairs leading to guest s.) Rates: $85 to $165 (for four guests in two rooms). Full kfast. Children accepted; no pets; no smoking; two night num stay. Near U.S.S. Constitution. *Represented by Bed Breakfast Associates, Bay Colony Ltd., Boston, MA.*

BAY VILLAGE. 1836 Federal style townhouse. Three guest rooms. Two share bath-and-a-half; one has private bath. All have working fireplaces and air conditioning. Rates: $80 to $105. Generous continental breakfast. Inquire about children; no pets; no smoking; no credit cards. Cats on premises. *Represented by Bed and Breakfast Associates, Bay Colony Ltd., Boston, MA.*

Left, the reception hall. Above, a private sun porch off the bedroom.

BOSTON—NORTH SHORE

A family home

Set on a fourteen acre estate, this rambling brown-shingled twenty-two room "cottage" is close to the fishing boats of Gloucester and the sailboat fleets of Manchester and scenic Rockport. There are acres of woodsy terrain to explore. It has its own tennis court, it is accessible to riding stables, and is a ten-minute walk from the beach.

Expansive and multi-leveled, the house is homey and casual. Old wood floors, comfortable plush period pieces, eyelit curtains, and large fireplaces abound. A sense of family history prevails: toys belonging to the father of the hostess, the host's father's art school diploma, over a hundred years old, passed down furniture and books, a large framed photo of the original Princeton Tiger belonging to the hostess's father (Princeton 1906).

Guests, essentially, have the run of the house.

Fires are always laid, ready to be lit, and a continental breakfast will be brought to the room upon request. A full breakfast is served near the fireplace in the ample dining room and, when weather permits, on the closed-in porch where wicker furniture overlooks the grounds.

Both guest rooms have old white iron bedsteads covered with delicate antique quilts. One room has an English charcoal grate fireplace and screened-in private deck overlooking a stand of hemlocks. The other chamber has a floral painted chest, oak desk, rag rug, and an antique white iron crib, in addition to two twin beds.

Framed on a wall a homily proclaims: "Mental health is our greatest wealth". The beauty of nature, an abiding sense of tranquility, sweet air, and the bliss of solitude here are all contributing factors.

NORTH SHORE. Twenty-two room Victorian estate on fourteen wooded acres. Open year-round. Two guest rooms each with private bath. Rates: $80 and $70 a room. Children welcome; pets welcome; no smoking; MasterCard/Visa/American Express. Close to Gloucester and Salem. Forty minutes to Boston. *Represented by Bed and Breakfast Associates, Bay Colony Ltd., Boston, MA.*

THE OVER LOOK INN

A haven of British hospitality

When sea captain Barnabas Chipman built his home in 1869, he sited it on the outer reaches of Cape Cod, close enough to the Atlantic Ocean to feel a part of the sea. More than a century later, Chipman's three-story Victorian clapboard home is a bed and breakfast inn and, sitting at the edge of the Cape Cod National Seashore and close to the Audubon Wildlife Sanctuary, it offers overnight guests proximity both to the sea and to the Cape's wild but delicate natural beauty.

Besides its great location, the Over Look Inn is a haven of traditional British hospitality personified by Scottish-born innkeepers Nan and Ian Aitchison, and their sons Mark and Clive. The Aitchisons painstakingly restored this vintage sea captain's home to a gleami..g finish, painting it soft butter yellow. They also diligently groom the inn's spacious lawn, which is wooded with mature

A brand new guest room.

shade trees that completely seclude it from neighbors.

The spirit of the British Isles is felt in the library, which is furnished with a leather couch and a working fireplace, because it is filled with books and memorabilia relating to Winston Churchill. And just down the hall, the Victorian billiards room seems a mandatory accoutrement to a proper British great house.

Continuing the tradition of their native island, the Aitchisons serve a full English breakfast each morning, often featuring the Scottish specialty *kedgeree*, a savory mixture of finnan haddie, rice, onions, chopped eggs, and raisins, sautéed in butter and served with a generous helping of mango chutney. At tea-time guests are supplied with traditional scones, hot and flaky and straight from the oven.

THE OVER LOOK INN, Rte. 6 (County Road), Eastham, Cape Cod, MA 02642; (508) 255-1886; Ian and Nan Aitchison, hosts, with son Mark. Open all year. Eight rooms with private baths. Rates: $80 double, with full English breakfast. No children; no pets; Visa/MasterCard/American Express. Victorian billiard room, croquet, bicycles, library on premises. Swimming, surfing, tennis, golf nearby. Excellent year-round dining nearby.

DIRECTIONS: 3 miles beyond Orleans Rotary, across from Salt Pond Visitor Center of Cape Cod.

The Billiard Room in the new section.

CHARLES HINCKLEY HOUSE

Where no detail is overlooked

"A small, intimate country inn where great expectations are quietly met." The Charles Hinckley House's brochure tells the truth. The house defines elegant simplicity. Hosts Miya and Les Patrick are consummate professionals. Their goal is to indulge each guest with exquisite perfection.

Situated on the Olde Kings Highway in a historic district, the Federal Colonial house bespeaks warmth, relaxation, and romance. Every room boasts a working fireplace, private bath, and period furnishings that blend well with the rich plums and blues of the decor.

No details are overlooked. Miya's wildflower garden provides fresh bouquets to complement the exotic blooms she specially orders in. Her breakfast is a succulent testament to her aesthetic sense; choosing a combination of tropical and local fruits, she presents a platter so pleasing that it was featured in full color in *Country Living* magazine. Homemade *creme fraiche* is available

Hosts Miya and Les Patrick.

as an alternative to cream or milk, and handmade chocolates accompany the turn-down service. Flannel sheets in winter and cotton ones in summer dress the beds, with covers of down comforters or handcrafted quilts which add just the right amount of coziness. Guests also enjoy scented soaps, toiletries, thick-piled cotton bath sheets.

Evenings are casual, with impromptu gatherings in the living room; however, privacy is as easily achievable. Honeymooners can expect a bottle of champagne and breakfast in bed, if they wish.

Miya and Les, as young as they are, have been pampering people for years—first at The Inn at Phillips Mill in New Hope, Pennsylvania, then at Graywillow, also on the Cape—but never as well as they do now. A stay here will surely prove their expertise.

CHARLES HINCKLEY HOUSE, Box 723, Barnstable Village, MA 02630; (617) 362-9924; Les and Miya Patrick, innkeepers. Open year round. Rates: $89 to $125 with full breakfast. Four guest rooms, all with private baths and working fireplaces. Children over 12 welcome; no pets; no smoking.

DIRECTIONS: from Rte. 3 take Rte. 6 to exit 6. At the end of the ramp, turn left. Turn right onto 6A at the stop sign (½ mile down the road). Go ½ mile more, and the house is on a slight rise to the left.

Very special breakfasts.

ASHLEY MANOR

Celebrating the colonial period

The warmth and elegance of the colonial period are celebrated at Ashley Manor, a bed and breakfast inn nestled in the heart of Cape Cod's historic Barnstable village. The inn is a softly weathered Cape shingle that grew, over three centuries, to become a small estate surrounded by two park-like acres. The original section of the house traces its beginnings to 1699, built when Barnstable was a tiny fishing settlement. Wide, worn floorboards gleaming with the patina of age; a massive hearth complete with beehive ovens; and a secret passage, used during the Revolutionary War, reveal the age and character of the inn's first incarnation.

Today, innkeepers Donald and Fay Bain take pride in their gracious home, and they are careful to fill it with furnishings that conform to its rich colonial atmosphere. The Bains give equal atten-

tion to providing life's graceful details, and to that end they fill rooms daily with fresh flowers; they offer guests an aperitif before dinner; and they stock bedside tables with a delightfully sinful cache of fine imported chocolates.

The inn contains six guest rooms, four of which are suites and five equipped with working fireplaces. The floorboards in several of the rooms sport original "Nantucket spackle" paint, which has been carefully preserved, and each room is decorated with fine traditional fabrics, furnishings, and wallcoverings. The end result is a thoroughly cozy and relaxing atmosphere.

Come the morning, guests find Donald hard at work in the kitchen preparing their morning feast. During summer months, breakfast at Ashley Manor is served *al fresco* on a brick terrace overlooking the inn's well-groomed grounds. When cool weather sets in, guests gather in the lovely old dining room. Here they relax in front of a blazing hearth and admire the Bains' collection of fine antique china displayed in charming corner cupboards.

ASHLEY MANOR, P.O. Box 856, 3660 Old Kings Highway (Rte. 6A), Barnstable, MA 02630; (508) 362-8044; Donald and Fay Bain, hosts. Open all year. Six rooms with private baths. Rates: $100 to $145, with full, multi course breakfast. Children over 14 welcome; no pets; Visa/MasterCard/American Express; French spoken. Croquet played on premises. Swimming, tennis, golf, antiquing, arts and crafts, other Cape Cod activities.

DIRECTIONS: take Rte. 6A East through village of Barnstable to light. Go straight through light for 9/10 miles to manor on left.

ISAIAH HALL INN

Nestled in a quiet Cape Cod village

Mirroring the gentle and relaxed spirit of the Cape, the Isaiah B. Hall bed and breakfast is warm-spirited and homey. This weathered shingle farmhouse, trimmed in white, and its attached white clapboard carriage barn, date back to 1857 when Isaiah Hall built himself a substantial homestead.

Innkeepers Marie and Dick Brophy are proud of their inn and they lavish it with plenty of tender loving care. They came to innkeeping from professional careers but, as Marie puts it, "It's more fun to make people happy." The Brophys' satisfaction results from their weaving a relaxed mood for guests to savor. They have filled this rambling old home with a colorful mix of antiques, vintage quilts, stained glass, oriental rugs, and handmade bric-a-brac. The living room, with its comfortable easy chairs and free-standing wood stove, and the wood-paneled game room, furnished with airy white wicker furniture and woven grass rugs,

beckon when the weather turns cold or inclement. Each of the nine guest rooms is cozy and simple; each is filled with antiques and compatible traditional pieces. After a good night's sleep, guests tuck into a substantial "expanded" continental breakfast of hot and cold cereals, fresh fruit, homebaked breads, and locally-produced jams and jellies. The site of this repast is the old-fashioned farmhouse dining room whose centerpiece is a long harvest table.

The inn, perfectly located in the bayside village of Dennis, nestles on a quiet side street just off the main road. It is an easy walk to all the attractions the village offers, which include: Corporation Beach; the Cape Playhouse and Cinema; a good selection of restaurants; antiques and crafts shops; and the Cape Museum of Fine Arts.

ISAIAH HALL B & B INN, 152 Whig Street, Dennis, MA 02638; (508) 385-9928; Marie and Dick Brophy, hosts. Open mid-March to mid-Nov. Eleven rooms, 10 with private baths. Rates: $48 to $78 double with extended continental breakfast. Children over 7 welcome; no pets; Visa/MasterCard/American Express accepted. Walking distance to beach, Cape playhouse, cinema, museum, village shopping, and fine restaurants. Badminton and croquet on premises.

DIRECTIONS: from Rte. 6 onto Cape take exit 8 and go left 1.2 miles to Rte. 6A and right for 3.4 miles to Dennis. Pass village green take left on Hope Lane to end and right on Whig to inn.

A rustic and comfortable bedroom in the Carriage Barn.

WINDAMAR HOUSE

Provincetown mix of antiques and art

At the tip of a twenty-five mile arc of beaches and windswept sand dunes, Provincetown, the terminus of Cape Cod, is a year-round resort of exceptional beauty. Summertime ushers in the carnival season. Two main thoroughfares, lined with art galleries, shops, museums, and restaurants, teem with tourists and sun worshippers. The contemplative beauty of the spring and fall attracts naturalists and artists. In winter, uncluttered by people and protected from Arctic temperatures by ocean currents, this spectacular landscape reveals its basic lines.

In any season Windamar House is a fine place to stay. Bette Adams' Cape colonial house sits in a quiet residential pocket just "this side" of Provincetown's commercial district. Windamar has a picket-fenced front yard, gardens, a terraced backyard filled with lawn furniture, and, most importantly, a private parking lot. In a town that can't expand geographically, all of the above are at a premium.

A guest suite.

Inside, the second-floor bedrooms range from a tiny cubbyhole to a suite with cathedral ceiling and a wall of glass. Besides single rooms, two fully equipped apartments are available for longer stays. Original art fills all available walls throughout the house, and bedrooms are an eclectic mix of antiques and comfortable period pieces.

Though Bette is always about, making sure the coffee pot is filled in the morning and seeing to the needs of her guests, she is not an intrusive presence. Free to barbecue in the backyard or sit for hours in the lounge (complete with "no-cook" kitchen), guests settle in and make themselves at home.

WINDAMAR HOUSE, 568 Commercial St., Provincetown, MA 02657; (617) 487-0599; Bette Adams, hostess. Some French spoken. Two houses joined together in the quiet east end of Provincetown. Open all year. Six guest rooms, sharing baths, and two fully equipped apartments. Rates $32 to $65 main house, according to season and room; apartments $50 per night off season, two-night minimum, $395 per week in season; rates include continental breakfast for rooms only. Excellent dining nearby. No children; no pets; no credit cards. Provincetown offers incomparable natural setting, year-round recreation, bird-watching, whale-watching.

DIRECTIONS: Take Cape Hwy. (Rte. 6) to Provincetown. Take first exit to water and turn right on 6A. At 'V' in road bear left onto Commercial St. Windamar House is ¼ mile ahead on right. Boats and flights available from Boston.

The stairway leading to the second-floor guest rooms.

The Capt. Harding Room has a fireplace and a bay window.

CAPTAIN DEXTER HOUSE

Island living at its best

Three blocks from the ferry, and the first home in the historic residential district of Vineyard Haven, The Captain Dexter House stands as a model of elegance, comfort, and convenience. Guests here can experience island living at its best—without billboards, fast-food franchises, not even stoplights—only picturesque seaside villages, quiet harbors, and glorious white sand beaches.

Martha's Vineyard is world-renowned for its natural beauty as well as its celebrities. The flat, straight southern shore provides miles of glacially carved, wave-dashed beach. The gentle curves on the island's other two sides lead into the calmer waters of Nantucket Sound to the east and Vineyard Sound to the west. North and center lies the year-round town which Stephen Veal and Julia Ross now call home.

The innkeepers like to describe the old sea captain's house as a "Federalized Victorian" with a peaked roof, bay windows, and side porch, but the interior recalls colonial times. A Williamsburg-style reproduction table assumes center stage in the dining room, flanked by Queen Anne-style chairs and beyond by a Sheraton breakfront and a Scottish grandfather clock that dates back to 1812. The far wall hosts two portraits painted in 1843, the same year that the house was built.

The eight well-kept guest rooms reflect the consideration put into the common rooms. Antiques and contemporary furnishings provide a pleasing mix that suits modern demands for comfort and charm.

THE CAPTAIN DEXTER HOUSE, Box 2457, 100 Main Street, Vineyard Haven, Martha's Vineyard, MA 02568; (617) 693-6564; Julia Ross and Stephen Veal, hosts. Open all year. Eight guest rooms, all with private baths, two with working fireplaces. Rates: $80 to $110 in season; $50 to $85 off-season; $15 for an additional person. Children over sixteen are welcome; no pets; smoking in guest rooms only; MasterCard/Visa/American Express. Continental breakfast. Guest refrigerator, beach towels, locked garage for bicycles. Watersports; horseback riding; summer theater; good restaurants nearby.

DIRECTIONS: Car reservations to and from Woods Hole should be made well in advance. Write or call the Parkers.

RHODE ISLAND

ADMIRAL FITZROY INN

An inn to
lift your spirits

An immaculate three-story, weathered-shingle hotel, the Admiral Fitzroy, one of the most enjoyable inns in Newport, is the brainchild of owner Jane Berriman and her husband Bruce. It is just one of three sister inns—the others being the Admiral Benbow and the Admiral Farragut—operated by the Berrimans, and each has its own character and style. The Berrimans are seasoned travelers who bring to innkeeping a refined sense of what the road-weary relish. At the Admiral Fitzroy this means all the amenities of an intimate, fine hotel with an abundance of grace notes usually reserved for home-style bed and breakfast inns.

The Admiral Fitzroy is tucked well away from the busy thoroughfare of Thames Street, but it offers wonderful views of the harbor and is perfectly located for walking the town. The inn is artfully conceived and is a showcase for fine craftsmanship, from the hand-carved Admiral Fitzroy plaque in the lobby (which was created by Bruce, a master woodcarver) to the hand painted, lacquered, and glazed wall treatments that add luster and richness to each room. Beds are dressed in fine linens, topped by plush down comforters. The innkeepers also attend to such welcome details as using fresh herbs in the breakfast omelet and offering guests fresh mint to flavor their coffee and tea.

The quality of service at the Admiral Fitzroy is top-notch. The inn's fine staff is congenial and one and all take great pride in working for this special inn.

ADMIRAL FITZROY INN, 398 Thames Street, Newport, RI 02840; (401) 847-4459; Jane Berriman, proprietor; Joan Fleming, host. Open Feb. 1 to Jan. 5. Eighteen rooms with private baths. Rates: winter $60 to $90; summer $95 to $120 with full breakfast. Children welcome; no pets; Visa/MasterCard/American Express. Newport activities, including sailing, swimming, golf. Extensive dining opportunities.

DIRECTIONS: located in downtown Newport, on the main street facing the harbor.

A top-floor bedroom, with balcony, overlooks Newport harbor.

First-floor formal parlor.

BRINLEY VICTORIAN INN

Unpretentious, well-tended, relaxed

On a quiet street off the beaten track, yet close to both the bustle of town and the mansions of Bellevue Avenue, the Brinley Victorian Inn is really two houses, a mansard-roofed Victorian frame and a smaller, adjoining counterpart. The parlor in the main house is formal and eye-pleasing, filled with Victorian settees, a rocker, and lace-draped tables, all in soft shades of green and cream. In the evening, guests congregate here, or in the game room at the rear of the house, comparing notes on the day's activities, preparing the next day's schedule, or relaxing over a game of cards. The overall atmosphere at the Brinley is unpretentious, friendly, well-tended, and relaxed.

The seventeen guest rooms are furnished with an easy mix of Victorian and contemporary pieces, and featured in each is one of owner Edwina Sebest's collection of antique miniature lamps and candlesticks. She and partner Amy Weintraub left high-powered jobs in Pittsburgh—Amy was a television writer and executive producer, Edwina a psychologist in private practice—to move to this city they both truly love. They operate a nursing home three blocks from the inn but are often at the Brinley to help out with chores and to visit with their guests.

THE BRINLEY VICTORIAN INN, 23 Brinley St., Newport, RI 02840; (401) 849-7645; Peter Carlisle, host; Dr. Edwina Sebest and Amy Weintraub, owners. Open year-round; Seventeen guest rooms; twelve with private baths. Two newly restored Victorian houses connected by walkway. Rates by room: winter, $55 to $75, summer, $70 to $95; $15 per extra person in room. Continental breakfast. No children under twelve; no pets; checks accepted. Extensive dining in area.

DIRECTIONS: from Newport/Jamestown bridge (Rte. 138), take downtown Newport exit. Go to third light and turn left onto Touro. At second light, turn left on Kay, and then right on Brinley. From north, take Rte. 114 into downtown. At movie theaters, bear left onto Touro and repeat above directions.

CLIFFSIDE INN

The grandeur of the Victorian age

Cliffside Inn captures the grandeur of the Victorian age with flowing curtains, bay windows, and commodious common rooms. This Second Empire summer cottage, which now stands among many beautiful houses in a peaceful residential district, once dominated the acreage. But even as times have changed, the luxury of the inn remains, as exemplified by the hallway floor's coat of arms, the last remnant of Cliffside's grand ballroom which burned down decades ago.

The ten guest rooms, all with private bath facilities, are imaginatively decorated. The coral and dark sea green of Miss Adele's Room is incorporated into a fireplace mantel that now functions as a headboard for the queen-sized bed. The Miss Beatrice Room, a favorite with newlyweds, is dressed in pinks and blues with bay windows and a Lincoln bed. Repeat visitors often ask for the light-filled Arbor Room situated off the porch. Its glass wall reminded one visitor of being in a botanical conservatory.

Cliffside has an unusual history. Built in 1880, the house served as a summer retreat for the governor of Maryland. Sixteen years later it became the site of a private preparatory school. The most famous denizen was Beatrice Pastorius Turner, who gained fame as a self-portrait artist and who painted the mother-daughter oil painting that hangs in the living room on the wall to the right of the piano. Her notoriety, however, came from her eccentricities. A recluse obsessed with youth, she walked into the town wearing Victorian clothes up until the 1940s.

Cliff Walk is about a ten-minute stroll away; the beach, even closer. All in all, Cliffside is a welcome addition to Newport's attractions.

CLIFFSIDE INN, 2 Seaview Avenue, Newport, RI 02840; (401) 847-1811; Kay Russell, innkeeper. Open May to October. Ten guest rooms, all with private baths. Rates: $71.50 to $93.50; slightly higher in season. The rate includes tax and a continental breakfast. Children over ten welcome; no pets; cats on premises.

DIRECTIONS: from I-95, take Rte. 138 over the Newport Bridge. Take a right onto Americas Cup Ave. and bear left onto Memorial Blvd. Take a right onto Cliff Ave. The inn is on the left, at the corner of Sea View Ave.

JAILHOUSE INN

A 1772 jail with modern amenities

If the urge to escape the daily grind causes guilt that borders on the criminal, Newport's Jail House Inn is the perfect destination for a quick getaway. The inn is thoroughly acquainted with offenders of every stripe, having served as Newport's house of detention since it was built in 1772. When the police moved their headquarters in 1985, Newport developer Don Glassie bought the property and converted the rambling edifice into a unique bed and breakfast inn.

The décor carries out a jail house theme, starting with the iron-barred check-in desk where guests are asked to give their incarceration date, anticipated parole date, and a description of their getaway car. "Workshirt" denim fabric covers each bed, and clothes the entire housekeeping staff. Sheets and towels are boldly striped, breakfast tables are set with classic tin, and the walls throughout are decorated with photos, paintings, artifacts, and memorabilia relating to the business of justice.

Guest accommodations range from rooms in

the "cell block" and "maximum security" to "solitary confinement." Each is comfortably furnished with sturdy, denim-upholstered furniture, which fits right in with the institutional grey carpeting and stark white walls. The inn deviates from the penal theme by equipping each bedroom with a television and telephone.

JAILHOUSE INN, 13 Marlborough Street, Newport, RI 02840; (401) 847-4638; Don Glassic, owner; Beth Hoban, Carol Panaccione, hosts. Open all year. Twenty-two rooms with private baths. Rates: seasonal, varying from $55 to $125 double, $5 for extra person. Children welcome; no pets; Visa/MasterCard/ American Express accepted; French, German spoken. Viewing the Newport mansions a must, plus swimming, tennis, boating, and eating seafood.

DIRECTIONS: from "Scenic Newport" exit turn right to second light and right again to light where fire station is on left. Turn left—inn is 2 blocks up on right. From Boston on Rte. 114 bear right at fork in road after police station and turn right onto Marlborough Street.

A spartan but chic bedroom on the second floor.

THE OLD DENNIS HOUSE

Bed and breakfast in Newport

Newport is many things to many people, from sailing mecca to the site of architectural wonders, from peerless colonial structures to ostentatious turn-of-the-century palaces.

The oldest section of Newport, known as The Point, is a quiet neighborhood filled with vintage homes, many of which were built in the mid-1700s when Newport was a major port city second only to Boston. Though Newport never fully recovered from the crippling destruction of the British occupation in 1776, the charm of The Point survived. Situated on the oldest street in Newport, the Old Dennis House stands out among these gracious survivors. Built in 1740 by Captain John Dennis, it serves as rectory for St. John's Episcopal Church and is one of Newport's finest bed and breakfast establishments.

Reverend Henry G. Turnbull had been rector of St. John's for over twenty years when a bed and breakfast registry persuaded him to open the spacious third floor of the rectory to guests. Besides the pleasure of meeting interesting people and offering comfortable accommodations to weary wayfarers (certainly a work of mercy), upkeep of the rectory was erased from the parish budget!

Each guest room is simple and charming with lots of exposed brickwork, several working fireplaces, and an eclectic mix of antiques. Located several blocks from the hubbub of Thames Street and Brick Market Place, the Old Dennis House is convenient to the bustling waterfront but feels a world removed.

THE OLD DENNIS HOUSE, 59 Washington St., Newport, RI 02840; (401) 846-1324; Rev. Henry G. Turnbull, host. Five guest rooms plus luxury suite in adjacent building; all with private baths. Working fireplaces, air conditioning, TV. Open year-round. Rates: double $65 to $85 in summer, $50 to $60 in winter. Continental breakfast. Children welcome; small pets allowed; smoking permitted; checks accepted.

DIRECTIONS: from Connecticut, cross Newport Bridge and take downtown Newport exit; 200 ft. off exit, turn right at light onto Van Zandt Ave. Go 3 blocks to Washington St. and turn left. Inn is about 7 blocks. From Boston, follow signs to Goat Island. At causeway to island, go 2 blocks north on Washington to corner of Poplar St.

St. John's Episcopal Church and the Rectory.

CONNECTICUT

INN AT CHAPEL WEST

New Haven extravaganza

Originally slated to become posh new office space, this eighteenth-century mansion has blossomed into a bed and breakfast on the revitalized upper Chapel Street. Once an unofficial Yale fraternity house, it is a fresh bouquet to the neighborhood and a symbol of New Haven's commitment to the restoration and reclamation of its heritage.

Eclectic in its décor, the guest rooms have faux marble door panels hinting at color schemes within. Room 34 has a cloudscape painted by connecticut muralist Peter Perry, a brass bedstead, a pine hope chest, and soft lavender, pink, and blue appointments. Room 21 has a lace-draped day bed and Austrian shades, while Room 11 has Laura Ashley fabrics, a pressed tin ceiling, a velvet paisley chair, and Victorian face masks. All of the beds, piled high with cushions and goose down pillows, are bedecked with ruffles and look wonderfully inviting. Some of the rooms have gas-lit fireplaces, and all of them have

Room 23, with poppy-colored walls and a working fireplace.

comfortable chairs, writing desks, telephones, and televisions. Bathrooms have pedestal sinks, blow dryers, and shower radios.

Continental breakfast, buffet-style, is served in the dining room and a catered dinner can be arranged. A tour of Yale, theater tickets to one of New Haven's many musical or dramatic offerings, transportation, and secretarial or babysitting services are happily attended to. The India Palace, Miya's, and Hot Tomatos, serving Indian, Japanese, and Italian food respectively, are literally a stone's throw away, as is an Art Deco diner across the way. Robert Henry's, a restaurant housed in Roger Sherman's former mansion a few blocks away, has awakened even the palates of Manhattanites.

In addition to housing visitors to Yale and people on business, the inn has already had its share of celebrities who were featured on the *Sally Jessy Raphael* show that originates in New Haven. Chuck Norris slept here, as did the moms of Cybil Shepard and Sylvester Stallone.

THE INN AT CHAPEL WEST, 1201 Chapel Street, New Haven, CT 06511; (203) 777-1201; Steven Schneider, host. Open all year. Ten guest rooms, all with private baths, telephone, color TV; some with fireplaces. Rates: $100 to $175, including continental breakfast. Children welcome; no pets; smoking allowed; all major credit cards. Handicap accessible. The inn is less than four blocks from Yale's Old Campus, New Haven Green, and minutes from New Haven's 30 plus pizza places.

DIRECTIONS: inn is located on Chapel Street, the main shopping street of downtown New Haven, leading to the green. Call for directions.

Room 33, with superb antique Victorian pieces.

PHOTOGRAPH BY WILLIAM SEITZ

RED BROOK INN

A colonial gem near Mystic Seaport

Sitting in a California Victorian house filled with a lifetime's collection of Early American antiques, Ruth Keyes came to the conclusion that she would never feel altogether at home in the West. An old fashioned girl at heart, she dreamt of Connecticut and a colonial village like Old Mystic. Within six months of her return to the East, she owned the beautiful 1770 Creary Homestead.

A recent and welcome addition expanding the inn is The Historic Haley Tavern, originally a stage coach stop. Restored and beautifully appointed, its rooms include The Ross Haley Chamber with antique furnishings and working fireplace, The Mary Virginia Chamber, a beautiful Early American room with canopy double bed, and The Victorian Nancy Creary Chamber with its own whirlpool tub.

Under Ruth's guardianship, the Red Brook Inn is a colonial showcase. Her collection of furniture and artifacts perfectly complements both the lines and the spirit of the house. All of the rooms are filled with period antiques, from the second-floor bedrooms with their blanket chests, highboys, and early lighting devices, to the first-floor keeping room with its original cooking fireplace, beehive oven, and iron crane and cookware. Each four-poster or canopied bed is coordinated with carefully chosen matching quilts and linens.

A full breakfast, served on the long harvest table in the keeping room, might include quiche, baked or fresh fruit, eggs Benedict, walnut waffles, or berry pancakes.

THE RED BROOK INN, Box 237, Rte. 184 at Wells Rd., Old Mystic, CT 06372; (203) 572-0349; Ruth Keyes, proprietor and host. Colonial gem built around 1770. Historic Haley Tavern circa 1740. Open year-round. Eleven guest rooms; all with private baths, eight with working fireplaces. Rates: $65–$150 per double room, including a full breakfast. No pets; no smoking in building; Visa/MasterCard. Mystic Seaport Museum, Mystic Aquarium, horseback riding, golf, sailing, submarine tour cruises on river, Coast Guard Academy nearby. Excellent dining in area.

DIRECTIONS: take I-95 to exit 89 (Allyn St.); go north 1½ miles to light (Rte. 184 Gold Star Hwy.). Turn right and go east ⅓ mile. Inn is on left.

THE PALMER INN

Turn-of-the-century mansion by-the-sea

Skillfully crafted by his shipbuilders, this turn-of-the-century eighteen-room seaside mansion was constructed for Robert Palmer, Jr., an owner of the largest wooden shipbuilding company on the East Coast in its day. Today the house carries on as an elegant inn, preserving the sea-faring history of its family and community.

Surrounded by rocky Connecticut shoreline, Noank, an old New England fishing village, is perched on a hillside peninsula at the mouth of the Mystic River. Unspoiled and seemingly untouched by modern ways, the narrow-street town has one inn, a restaurant, a post office, a couple

A seaside mansion crafted by shipwrights.

of stores and art galleries, and well-kept old colonial homes. A white church steeple rises from a hilltop as in a painting.

Tastefully furnished with Victorian furniture, period wallpapers, brass fixtures, and antique appointments, it boasts a good measure of family heirlooms. Original and unusual stained glass windows add drama to the rooms. Lush flowers and herb gardens adorn the spacious grounds.

As you enter the magnificent mahogany main hall of the Palmer Inn, you leave all of your earthly cares behind. And you only know that tonight you will be *a-sleepin' by the sea.*

THE PALMER INN, 25 Church Street, Noank, CT 06340; (203) 572-9000; Donald and Patricia Cornish, hosts. Open year round. Six spacious guest rooms with private and shared baths. Rates: $80 to $135; includes pleasant continental breakfast. Children sixteen and over; no pets; no smoking in guest rooms or dining area; Visa/MasterCard. Dachshunds on premises. Within walking distance of tennis, sailing, art galleries, swimming, and fine lobster house.

DIRECTIONS: take I-95 to exit 89, Allyn Street. From north take a right (and from south a left) and travel through two traffic lights across Rte. 1 onto West Mystic Avenue to stop sign. Turn right onto Noank Road (Route 215) and travel 1.7 miles to stop sign. Turn left onto Mosher, past fire house, and turn left onto Main Street. Go 1 block and left onto Church. Tall hedges surround inn. Guest parking in back of inn.

BISHOP'S GATE INN

Theater people in a theater town

Perched on the banks of the Connecticut River, the grand proportions of the Goodspeed Opera House rise in sharp contrast to the surrounding tiny town of East Haddam. The Goodspeed produces musical comedy revivals and one new production a year—including the birth of such hits as *Man of La Mancha, Shenandoah,* and *Annie.*

Bishop's Gate Inn, located in the center of town, is a gem. Established by Julie Bishop, who worked with the Goodspeed actors, the theatrical tradition is being carried on by current innkeepers Molly and Dan Swartz. Both have spent years in the theater, Molly in costuming in Manhattan and Dan running a performing arts center in Brooklyn. This link to the theatrical arts is immediately apparent upon entering the home, where guests come upon the breakfast room with its sturdy harvest table. Above the table hangs a gallery of acting friends of the Swartzes' who have stayed at the inn, as well as a framed theater poster.

The Jenny Lind Room.

Besides the full breakfast, which might include stuffed French toast, buttermilk pancakes, or hearty egg dishes, the innkeepers offer guests dinner if they request it in advance. These romantic candlelit dinners, served on tables-for-two before a blazing fire, show off Molly's flair for delicate Northern Italian cuisine.

Each bedroom is completely comfortable and most display handsome early American furnishings and accessories. One favorite bed chamber displays a pencil-post four-poster bed draped with fishnet canopy and covered with a colonial-style waffle-weave bedspread. The Director's Suite is dramatic with its beamed cathedral ceiling, private balcony, and "Hollywood" bathroom complete with double sinks, sauna, and sitting area.

BISHOP'S GATE INN, Goodspeed Landing, East Haddam, CT 06423; (203) 873-1677; Dan and Molly Swartz, hosts. Colonial built in 1818 and filled with family antiques. Six guest rooms all with private baths. Open year-round: $75–95 double. No children under six, no pets; Visa/MasterCard, checks accepted. Hearty full breakfast; picnic lunches can be arranged. Many wonderful restaurants a short drive away. Goodspeed Opera House, museums, state parks, Connecticut River cruises, airstrip on riverbank.

DIRECTIONS: from New York City, Providence, or Boston, take Connecticut Tnpke. (I-95) to exit 69 to Rte. 9. From Rte. 9 take exit 7 to East Haddam. Cross bridge and go straight on Rte. 82 for 1 block. Inn driveway is on left.

An exquisite piece of marquetry furniture.

STONECROFT INN

Refined conviviality

Before coming East and acquiring the Stonecroft Inn, Bonnie Baskin had already meticulously restored and run a Victorian inn in Seattle, Washington. Shopping for an inn in Connecticut, her practiced eye was smitten by the architectural integrity, the age, and the feel of the 1832 clapboard Stonecroft Inn. Built by Austin Shaler, a prosperous blacksmith, it is set on a grassy hillside in East Haddam's historic district.

Bonnie, not a believer in "museum pieces" that cannot be used for entertaining, has enhanced the inn with her family's antique pieces: a Victorian rosewood sofa brought over from England by her sea captain grandfather; a small leaded-glass Welsh cabinet crafted by her great-grandfather and brought over from Ireland; a pine boot-box made for her grandmother to keep her boots

in when she was a girl—and now placed in front of one of the antique beds.

A real cigar store Indian presides over the inviting dining room. Apple Pan Dowdy, nutkin muffins, eggs Benedict, a cheese soufflé, or a mushroom and bacon quiche may be waiting in the wings. And coffee on the porch includes a spectacular view of the Connecticut River Valley and forested hillsides of East Haddam.

As a former drama major, Bonnie has a keen sense of the arts and believes in partaking of the inngoing experience and becoming a part of it. Parents of actors and playgoers to the nearby Goodspeed Opera House as well as visitors to the steam train in Essex and to Gillette Castle will find the Stonecroft Inn a happy ending to the day.

STONECROFT INN, 17 Main St., East Haddam, CT 06423; (203) 873-1754; Bonnie Baskin, host. Federal-style clapboard house built as a private residence in 1832. Open year-round. Five guest rooms, all with private baths; some with fireplaces. Rates: $75 to $85. No children under 12; no pets; no credit cards accepted. Canoeing, theatres, and antiquing attract most visitors.

DIRECTIONS: from I-95 take exit 69 to Rte. 9 (exit 7). Follow the signs for the Goodspeed Opera House. The inn is four buildings up from the Goodspeed.

WEST LANE INN

Sample the good life in a private mansion

A New England getaway close to city bustle, the West Lane Inn in historic Ridgefield, Connecticut, is just fifty miles from New York City. This bed and breakfast inn contains more rooms than most, so guests don't always share their morning muffin and coffee with owner Maureen Mayer. But they enjoy the solid comforts evident throughout this grand, early nineteenth-century mansion. Among the amenities generally found only in fine hotels are thick padded carpets and a double thickness of door between adjoining rooms, which helps maintain the prevailing sense of quiet and privacy. Bathrooms are equipped with heated towel racks, full-length mirrors, and, in some cases, bidets. An adjoining house, called the Cottage, contains suites with service kitchens and private decks that open onto a vast expanse of well-manicured lawn. A simple room service menu, an optional full breakfast, king and queen-size beds, a tennis court, and one-day laundry and dry cleaning service make the West Lane Inn a welcome haven for tired wayfarers and business travelers.

WEST LANE INN, 22 West Lane, Ridgefield, CT 06877; (203) 438-7323; Maureen Mayer, hostess. Former private mansion invites guests to sample the good life. Open all year. Fourteen guest rooms in main house, two with working fireplaces; six suites in rear cottage, all with private baths. Rates: $90 single, $110 double, including continental breakfast; full breakfast available for extra charge. Good dining in area. Children welcome, cribs and playpens available; no pets; major credit cards; no checks. Ridgefield offers Revolutionary War sites, tours, museums; cross-country and downhill skiing.

DIRECTIONS: from NYC, take the FDR to the Major Deegan to Saw Mill Pkwy. Stay on Saw Mill to end and exit onto Rte. 35 going east. Drive approximately 12 miles to Ridgefield. Inn is on Rte. 35.

A portrait of the son of the original owner hangs in the stairwell.

BUTTERNUT FARM

An impressive, small museum

Butternut Farm in Glastonbury, Connecticut, is an especially fine example of pre-Revolutionary architecture. The oldest section of the house was built by Jonathan Hale in 1720, a well-to-do gentleman with an eye for fine moldings and a feel for proportion—rare commodities in early homes. By the mid-1700s, a keeping room, "borning room," buttery, and extra bedchambers were added as Hale's family grew.

Present owner Don Reid is a faithful steward to this architectural gem. He loves early American antiques and has collected many excellent examples from the period, including an antique pencil post canopied bed, an exquisite cherry highboy, and pre-Revolutionary bottles and Bennington pottery marbles.

The keeping room has beams bedecked with drying herbs and flowers. An antique settle and variety of chairs surround the large hearth, whose magnitude is completely overshadowed by the second fireplace found in the adjoining dining room. This brick hearth, of mammoth proportions, is teamed up with an oversized antique dining table and bannister-back chairs. An oil painting of Jonathan Hale's son is prominently displayed.

Guest rooms upstairs are decorated with wing-back chairs, wooden chests, and antique hat-boxes. Museum quality, hand-hooked rugs brighten softly gleaming, wide-plank pine floorboards.

Don Reid is a soft-spoken and intellectual man who takes great pride in the home he has created. Continuously occupied since its construction, the house shares its charm with appreciative guests. A carefully tended museum of Americana, this inn is like another world—one that should be visited and revisited to enjoy its many facets.

BUTTERNUT FARM, 1654 Main St., Glastonbury, CT 06033; (203) 633-7197; Don Reid, host. Elegant house built in 1720, with a wealth of interesting architecture detail. Open year-round. Two guest rooms, with two shared baths; two apartments with private baths. Rates: $55 single, $60 and $75 double. Full breakfast. Checks accepted; no pets; smoking discouraged. Good dining in town and in adjoining Hartford.

DIRECTIONS: take I-84 or I-91 to Rte. 2 exit. Follow Rte. 2 and take exit 8; go right toward Glastonbury Center. Drive to Main St. and turn left. Drive 1.6 miles, and inn is on left.

Described as Tudor-Bavarian in style.

MANOR HOUSE

One of Connecticut's finest

A beautiful turn-of-the-century mansion, the Manor House in Norfolk, Connecticut, with wood paneled walls and huge stone fireplaces, is the setting for a bed and breakfast inn *par excellence*. Described by some as the most elegant bed and breakfast in Connecticut, the Manor House is the focus of a number of other activities as well.

The innkeepers, who love classical music, have formed a novel partnership with neighbors Carl and Marilee Dudash, who make beautifully decorated harpsichords. The result is the Norfolk Early Music Society and occasional concerts at the Manor House during the winter season, when nearby Tanglewood and Music Mountain are quiescent.

Horse-drawn sleigh and carriage rides are provided for guests during the appropriate season

after breakfasts of fresh farm eggs, bacon, orange waffles, blueberry pancakes, french toast, home-made breads, muffins, and coffee.

Diane and Henry Tremblay are new innkeepers who "fell in love at first sight" with the fine old eighteen-room manor. Since there was room enough for both their large family and guests as well, they decided to move in.

The house was built in 1898 by Charles Spofford, designer of London's Underground and son of Ainsworth Rand Spofford, head of the Library of Congress under President Lincoln. The interior is distinctly Victorian, with elegantly carved furniture, ornate fixtures, leaded glass windows, and billowy white curtains.

MANOR HOUSE. P.O. Box 701, Maple Avenue, Norfolk, C 06058; (203) 542-5690; Diane and Henry Tremblay, hosts. Ope all year. Eight guest rooms, most with private baths, some wit fireplaces and private balconies. Rates: $60-$75 single, $65 $130 double; includes full breakfast. Children over 12 welcome no pets (boarding kennels nearby). Yale Summer School of Musi and Art an annual event in Norfolk, as well as crafts, antiques theater, and golf.

DIRECTIONS: take I-84 to exit for Rte. 8 north at Waterbur Conn. Go north to end of Rte. 8 at Winsted and take Rte. 4 west to Norfolk and Maple Avenue. From Massachusetts tak Turnpike west to Rte. 7 exit and go south to Canaan and ea on Rte. 44 to Norfolk.

NEW YORK

One of the premier bed and breakfasts

This restored stone farmhouse has been used as a Bed and Breakfast ever since it was built in about 1780. Located in an area known as "rest plaus," Dutch for "the rest place," it was a stopover for travelers near a ford in the Roundout River.

Furnished with eighteenth-century country-style antiques and situated on sixteen acres of verdant lawn, it overlooks farms, woods, and mountains. There are herb, rose, and flower gardens and an inviting swimming pool. Guests relax on the first floor of the farmhouse with its colorfully stenciled rooms, its Rumford fireplaces, solarium, and green house with hot tub. Five early American guest rooms, some with private baths, are available year round.

Doug Baker and Linda Delgado, teachers at a local college, are seasoned hosts. Doug, a biologist, loves talking about the local wildlife, restoration, and antiques. Linda, who is fluent in Spanish, is a history buff. Both are gifted cooks, and serve a full gourmet breakfast that includes freshly baked pastries, home grown fruits and vegetables, and their own jams and preserves.

The Shawangunk Mountain Ridge is a magnificent backdrop for the Baker's stone house. Cross-country ski trails and hiking trails abound, and the variety and number of fine restaurants is extraordinary. This area has become a mecca for serious epicures.

BAKER'S BED AND BREAKFAST, RD 2, Box 80, Stone Ridge, NY 12484; (914) 687-9795; Doug Baker and Linda Delgado, hosts. Six rooms with private and shared baths in a 1700s stone house. Open all year. Rates: $68 single, $85 double; includes an elegant breakfast of wonderful breads and creative egg specialties served at 9:30 A.M. Two-night minimum required on weekends; overnight guests mid-week. No children under 12; no pets; all credit cards; checks accepted. Non-smokers preferred but a considerate smoker would be acceptable.

DIRECTIONS: New York State Thruway (I-87) to New Paltz, exit 18. Drive west on Route 299 into New Paltz, turning right onto Rte. 32. Head north for about 6 miles and turn left onto Rte. 213. Proceed through High Falls and turn left onto Rte. 209. Go exactly 1 mile and take the second left off Rte. 209, which is Old Kings Highway; Baker's is midway down the hill on the right.

THE OLDE POST INN

Live music
on weekends

Nestled on the banks of the Hudson River, the town of Cold Spring basks in the beauty of the Palisades across the water. This village is an interesting mix of "local color" and city folk who were lured to the town for its lovely architecture and glorious setting. Among such new residents are Carole Zeller and George Argila. Their home, The Olde Post Inn, sits on a prominent corner of Main Street, two blocks from the river, and is one of the most successful restorations in the village. Built in 1820 as a post office and customs house, the building is on the National Historic Register.

The first floor of this cozy bed and breakfast serves as breakfast room and sitting room. It has open beamwork, hardwood floors, an antique sideboard, comfortable furniture, and a wall of glass that faces the backyard and patio, washing the beautiful woodwork with soft light. Carole collects American crafts, while George, a graduate of the Julliard School of Music, has opened a small cabaret in the basement. In the process of

converting this unused basement space, George and Carole discovered a beehive fireplace, which sets the tone for the tavern. With its own separate entrance, no traffic flows from tavern to inn, except for those guests who spend the evening listening to music. George and other gifted, local musicians play on weekends—and no heavy rock is allowed.

It seems that at least half of Cold Spring is composed of antiques shops and other interesting stores. Besides shopping, visitors can tour the Chapel of Our Lady, an 1834 Greek Revival chapel, which was reproduced in Currier and Ives prints over a century ago, and the elegant eighteenth-century mansion called Boscobel. A short drive away are the Franklin D. Roosevelt National Historic Site and the fifty-room Vanderbilt mansion.

THE OLDE POST INN, 43 Main St., Cold Spring, NY 10516; (914) 265-2510; Carole Zeller and George Argila, hosts. 1820 Federal-style inn was once a post office and customs house. Open all year. Six guest rooms decorated in simple American traditional, with shared baths. Rates $55 to $65 per room, including continental breakfast with homemade breads. Excellent dining nearby. Older children welcome; no pets; Visa/MasterCard. Tavern downstairs features live music on weekend nights.

DIRECTIONS: from west side of Hudson take Palisades Pkwy. to Bear Mt. Bridge. Turn left on Rte. 9D and proceed into Cold Spring. Turn left at light onto Main St. From NYC, take Taconic Pkwy. to Rte. 301, Cold Spring exit. Also from NYC, take Rte. 9 to Rte. 301, which becomes Main St. at Cold Spring.

Left, the view from the breakfast room into the living room.

CAPTAIN SCHOONMAKER'S

astronomical
reakfasts

1760 stone house on the Kriegs' property is main house, but is only one of three accommating structures that comprise Captain oonmaker's. Just beyond the driveway sits a msically restored barn, where the most asked r rooms look out over the brook. The other t often-requested rooms are hidden away down street in the old canal lock-tender's quarters. sts have to walk the half mile from the canal cottage to the main house, but it's a welcome vity after Julia Krieg's amazingly ample break-

alkative and perky, hostess Julia won't take or an answer. Her guests groan with surfeited ght by the fourth course at breakfast. Satur s usual menu begins with broiled grapefruit moves on to an herb-cheese soufflé accom ied by sausage almost candied with New York le syrup. The meal continues with a halo of cot and honey danish. Is breakfast over? No; theatrical timing, Julia again appears: this with cherry strudel. Hence, the groan.

AIN SCHOONMAKER'S 1760 STONE HOUSE, Box 37, Route High Falls, NY 12440; (914) 687-7946; Sam and Julia , hosts. Open year-round. Three guests rooms in the main house, four rooms in the carriage house/barn, four rooms e Towpath House; all with private or shared baths. Two s with fireplace. Rates: $65 and $75. Full breakfast. Children me during the week, over 6 only, on weekends; no pets; redit cards. Hiking, boating, tubing, swimming, scuba g, horseback riding, golf, wineries, summer theater nearby. RECTIONS: from Kingston take Rte. 209W to Ellenville to to Rosendale (left turn), about 3 miles to the house, which the right. Sam will pick guests up at the bus station in ndale.

MAPLE SHADE
BED & BREAKFAST

A country oasis

Hidden away in some of New York's most beautiful countryside, Cooperstown sits on the shores of scenic Lake Otsego. There's nothing pretentious about this sophisticated back-country oasis. The small shopping district is well-organized to fend off insensitive developers, and so Main Street flourishes as it did years ago with stores and a 1920s movie theatre. Even the National Baseball Hall of Fame hasn't intruded on the town's quiet sense of pride and practicality.

Judge William Cooper settled here in 1786 and built the village's first two log structures. His son, James Fenimore, immortalized the area in his books.

The tone is casual and friendly. White and pastel colors define the American country theme, and set off the slate blue carpeting. Old oak, new brass, and wicker blend together into a pleasing package presided over by congenial hosts Robert and Linda Crampton, natives of the area.

MAPLE SHADE BED AND BREAKFST, R.D. #1, Box 105A, Milford, NY 13807; (607) 547-9530; Robert and Linda Crampton, hosts. Open all year. Three guest rooms share two baths; one suite has private bath. Rates: $48 to $60; $5 additional per person; includes hearty breakfast. Children allowed, no pets; no smoking; Visa/MasterCard. Good restaurants are abundant.
    DIRECTIONS: from the south, take the New York State Thruway to exit 21 (Catskill) to Rte. 145 north. Turn onto Rte. 20 west, then Rte. 28 south through Cooperstown. The inn is four miles from town, on the right. From I-88, take Rte. 28 north. The inn is on the left.

The house is colorful, gay, and fanciful.

UJJALA'S BED & BREAKFAST

A bit of California in upstate New York

Ujjala's Bed and Breakfast vibrates with a California sensibility. Her charming Victorian frame cottage sits amidst a grove of apple, pear, and quince trees, and is painted in luscious hues of lilac, periwinkle, and plum. Ujjala renovated her home and added skylights, contemporary stained glass, lots of plants, whimsical ceramics, and flowers.

The focus at Ujjala's is on health. With a background in "body therapy"—Shiatsu and deep-relaxation therapy—she has given courses in stress management to university students and corporate business people, and she was filmed for the television special "The Body Human." Ujjala is also an able cook who specializes in "vegetarian gourmet" cuisine. Her full breakfast includes homemade whole grain breads, fresh fruits, and eggs, and she goes out of her way to accommodate people on special diets. If you've always wanted to cleanse your system with a fast or a special diet, a stay at Ujjala's may be in order. Link a well-balanced and healthful diet with Ujjala's therapy and you can come away from this bed and breakfast feeling like a brand new person.

UJJALA'S BED AND BREAKFAST, 2 Forest Glen Rd., New Paltz, NY 12561; (914) 255-6360; Ujjala Schwartz, hostess. Open all year. Five guest rooms with private and shared baths. Rates $50 to $75 double, including full breakfast. Afternoon tea and coffee, sherry in winter. Excellent dining nearby. Inquire about children; no pets; smoking discouraged; no credit cards. Inn offers exercise and relaxation therapy programs.

DIRECTIONS: from N.Y. State Thruway, take New Paltz Exit 18. Go left on Rte. 299 into town and turn left at light onto Rte. 208 S. Drive 3½ miles, passing Dressel Farm on right, take second right onto Forest Glen Rd. Ujjala's is driveway on left.

STAGECOACH INN

Its own brand of romance

Bustling Lake Placid Village lies tucked between two shimmering bodies of water. Shallow and tranquil Mirror Lake laps up to the town's center. Just a few miles north, Lake Placid serves as the village's reservoir, reaching spring-fed depths of over 300 feet—an angler's paradise with native fish as well as upwards of 10,000 rainbow and lake trout stocked by the state each year.

Sports activities are a large part of village life. Many of the 1980 Winter Olympic structures continue to bring in world-class championships throughout the year.

The 1833 clapboard Stagecoach Inn sits two miles northwest of the ski jumps on a back street away from traffic and village noise. Rustic and casual, the inn delivers its own brand of romance to its guests. Warmed by a fireplace, the two-tory cathedral-ceilinged living room invites sitting back and enjoying the Adirondack-style

details that once marked an era of extravagant parties and stimulating conversation. Yellow birch logs and twigs form the mantel, bookshelves, and support beams, as well as an imposing banister that leads to a second floor balcony.

The view down to the living room makes a still life *extraordinaire*. A deer head rests comfortably above the fireplace, a working Mason and Hamlin organ stands to the left, and on the side wall crossed snowshoes hang over framed photos of former innkeepers Mr. and Mrs. Lyons.

The other common area, the dining room, encloses its visitors with Georgia pine on the walls, ceiling, and floors. A cozy fire reflects in the wood's sheen, casting an amber radiance on the morning meal—a perfect touch to start any day.

THE STAGECOACH INN, Old Military Road, Lake Placid, NY 12946; (518) 523-9474; Peter Moreau, inn owner; Lin Witte, innkeeper. Open all year. Nine cozy guest rooms, five with private baths, two with fireplaces. Rates: $40 to $45, single; $50 to $70, double; $10 for an additional person. Children over 10 welcome; inquire about pets. Sports activities nearby include golf, hiking, rock climbing, trout fishing, horseback riding. Skating school ice shows every Saturday night in session; Mercedes Circuit horse show in summer.

DIRECTIONS: from the Adirondack Northway (Rte. 87), take Rte. 73N for 30 miles. Bear left just past the ski jumps (where the Saranac Lake sign is pointing). The inn is about two miles down on the left.

J. P. SILL HOUSE

A showcase of wallpapers

Formal elegance betrays a studied warmth in the J.P. Sill House, a showcase of impeccably designed and printed wallpapers. The handscreened "room sets" may include as many as seven different yet harmonious patterns. All are based on original works by turn-of-the-century artists. Innkeeper Joyce Bohlman discovered the California firm of Bradbury & Bradbury from a newspaper article; an inquiry and a visit to the firm convinced her to paper the house with these carefully chosen designs. Hiring a paperhanger was no problem, either; one of Joyce's brothers is a professional. The results are spectacular.

The green-hued formal dining room carries an Eastlake frieze paper initially reproduced for the Cameron-Stanford House in Oakland, California; the fill paper, a graceful willow pattern, is attributed to William Morris. Both become richer when sunlight filters in through the room's French doors that open onto one of the inn's porches.

Joyce kept pieces of the wallpapers with her for six months wherever she traveled, buying

More Bradbury and Bradbury wallpaper, in the Downstairs Parlor, left, and in the Peacock Room, above.

material and accessories to fit the beautifully appointed rooms, all of which are furnished with antiques to match the ambiance of the papers: an Eastlake bed stands at counterpoint to the green marble fireplace in the Master Bedroom; a brass and white-iron bed complements the soft peach and blue of the Shell Room. Linens and lace add to the details.

The house seduces its guests. A long tin bathtub invites visitors to take a luxurious break—bath powder already provided. Seasonal fruit baskets or homemade sweets adorn the rooms as appropriately as the objets d'arts, and potpourri scents the air.

Expect the same quality of attention at breakfast. Simply prepared gourmet fare comes presented on china. White linen napkins and silver service complete this unabashed indulgence.

THE J.P. SILL HOUSE, 63 Chestnut St., Cooperstown, NY 13326; (607) 547-2633; Joyce Bohlman, innkeeper. Open all year. 1894 Italiante Victorian on state and national historic registers. Five guest rooms share two baths. Rates: $50 to $65, slightly higher on Hall of Fame Weekend. Two-night minimum for summer weekends; four-night minimum for Hall of Fame Weekend. Full, elegant breakfast. No pets, kennel nearby; no children under 13; no smoking. Year-round sports activities: Lake Otsego; Baseball Hall of Fame; Farmer's Museum; Fenimore House; antiquing, auctions, summer theatre, and opera.

DIRECTIONS: once in Cooperstown, ask inn for location of the house.

THE ROSE MANSION AND GARDENS

Rochester's hidden treasure

The inn, Rochester's hidden treasure, stands behind a towering stone wall, and includes an impressive garden designed by George Ellwanger, a prominent nurseryman who owned the house.

Ellwanger planted the grounds with the idea that the gardens would serve as a continuation of the house—as an outdoor room. The gravel paths offer a rich variety, from boxwood hedge borders to a lavender walk with a weeping cherry tree, copper beech trees, and old pear trees. In all, more than seventy-five kinds of flowering and green plants are represented, including some beds of rare unusual roses.

The formal but welcoming house is as grand as its gardens. At the landing midway between the first and second floors is an 1887 Hook and Hastings pipe organ tucked into the wall; the pipes rise monumentally up to the high ceiling. The organ inspired Stephen and Jeanne Ferranti to organize a Christmas spectacular. The event, which takes place in even-numbered years, has featured the German Youth Orchestra and high-lighted a nineteen-foot tree in the great hall landing, with children forming a line up the stairs, each one holding a candle.

Most of the year, however, a refined quiet reigns in the house. A Chickering grand piano and a chess set provide an evening's entertainment in the Victorian Great Room, which still displays a silk-and-cotton blend beige tapestry wallpaper, a detail lost in most renovations. French doors open onto the porch that fronts the garden, and another pair leads into the dining room where an elegant continental breakfast is served.

Each of the ten spacious guest rooms is named for a rose, and all are comfortably and aristo-cratically furnished with antiques.

THE ROSE MANSION AND GARDENS, 625 Mt. Hope Ave., Rochester, NY 14620; (716) 546-5426; Stephen and Jeanne Ferranti, innkeepers. Open all year. Some French and Spanish spoken. Ten guest rooms, three with fireplaces; suite arrangements available. All with private baths. Rates: $77 to $105, single; $82 to $115, double; additional person, $10. Continental breakfast included. Children over 11 welcome; no pets; smoking in the guest rooms only. American Express/MasterCard/Visa.

DIRECTIONS: from east and Thruway exit 45, take Rte. 490 west. Follow sign for Rte. 390 north, Airport. Bear left. Take exit 16 (Rte. 15 and 15A). From exit proceed straight, follow sign for Rte. 15 north. Turn right onto Rte. 15. Pass Elmwood Ave; continue about 1 mile. Rose Mansion and Gardens is on the left. From the south and Thruway exit 46, take Rte. 390 north to exit 16. Follow directions above.

Swarthmore, and Camelot sitting room beyond—the names of roses.

ROSEWOOD INN

Unique character and charm

This 1855 Greek Revival mansion was transformed into an English Tudor in 1917 and is now a bed and breakfast, presided over by popular local newspaper editor Dick Peer, his wife Winnie, and daughter Amy. It is a first-class hostelry in the finest tradition.

Six guest rooms, named after popular figures, offer their own unique character and charm. The Jenny Lind Room features sheet music and programs from the Swedish Nightingale's concerts; the Herman Melville Room, Gloucester whaling prints and a harpoon on the mantel; the Charles Dana Gibson Room, Gibson Girl prints and Eastlake furniture.

The Corning Glass Museum, within walking distance of Rosewood Inn, houses the most extensive glass collection in the world. On display are ancient Egyptian, Roman, Venetian, and Persian glass, and a vast Tiffany window of a scene overlooking the Hudson.

The Rockwell Museum, also nearby, features the largest collection of Western art in the eastern United States.

ROSEWOOD INN, 134 East First St., Corning, NY 14830; (607) 962-3253; Winnie, Dick, and Amy Peer, hosts. Open all year. Six guest rooms, four with private baths. Rates $45 to $85. Includes full breakfast. Children welcome; inquire about pets; smoking on side porch; Visa/MasterCard/Diners Club. Scenic Finger Lakes, Watkins Glen, auto racing, wineries, Ithaca and its universities within a short drive.

DIRECTIONS: take Rte. 17 through downtown Corning. East First Street parallels Rte. 17 one block to the south.

The Jenny Lind Room.

PHOTOGRAPHS COURTESY ROSEWOOD INN

JAMES RUSSELL WEBSTER INN

Two grand, palatial suites

uilt by one of the Webster brothers of dictionary me, and graced by a terraced courtyard, this nately-decorated Greek Revival mansion is set the glorious Finger Lakes region of New York ate.

Two grand palatial suites in the James Russell ebster Mansion offer everything. Private en- nces, luxurious canopied beds, marble baths d fireplaces, black-and-white harlequin floors— exude elegance. Museum-quality collections ill over throughout and into the suites. For cat vers there are more than 600 cat figurines— usical cats, a marching band, ball-playing cats, om cats and kittens. Rare European clocks— andfather, double fusée chain bracket, autom- on, and lantern clocks—are on display. And intings by noted artists of the eighteenth and neteenth centuries are hung throughout the inn. A breakfast of freshly-baked sticky buns, breads,

t, one of the two opulent suites.

pastries, fruits, imported cheeses, coffee, and tea are served on antique china with silver appoint- ments, while a full gourmet breakfast is available at extra charge. Eggs Florentine, Quiche Lorraine, Nova Scotia, and home-baked bagels highlight the fare.

Candlelight dinners in the palatial dining room or in the summer dining house are easily arranged in advance. Gourmet-cook owner Barbara Cohen can furnish exquisite Veal Orloff, Poulet Dan- nielle, succulent glazed. duckling, and lobster overflowing with crabmeat. Desserts are too mouthwatering to mention in passing.

Local attractions include Seneca Falls, the Rose Hill Mansion with its boxwood gardens, the only Women's Rights National Park in the world, the Women's Hall of Fame, and a Scythe Tree, where farm boys hung their scythes as they marched off to the Civil War.

THE HISTORIC JAMES RUSSELL WEBSTER MANSION INN, 115 East Main Street, Waterloo, NY 13165; (315) 539-3032; Leonard and Barbara Cohen, hosts. Two grand palatial suites with enormous half moon windows, carved fan shaped mouldings, 12-foot 18th century Georgian doors, marble fireplaces, and marble baths. Rates: $180.00 per night double. Dinners $60 to $70 per person. Gourmet continental breakfast included, full gourmet breakfast extra. No children; no pets; no smoking; Visa/MasterCard. Delightful pet cats on premises. In the heart of the Finger Lakes country with eleven lakes, a thousand waterfalls, and fabulous fall foliage.

DIRECTIONS: Between Geneva and Seneca Falls. Exit 41 on New York State Thruway. Call for directions.

NYC—GREENWICH VILLAGE

Sophisticated décor

n addition to a panoramic view of Lobro, the newly developed part of lower Broadway, this heart-of-the-village bed and breakfast is a fifteen minute jaunt to Chinatown and less than that to Little Italy and the lower east side. Bordering on Soho and its art galleries, boutiques, wearable art, and exciting new restaurants, the bed and breakfast is a stone's throw away from bakery/cafés serving such fare as sfogliatella, napoleons, and pignoli tarts.

The airy cheerful apartment has two guestrooms: a pretty floral bedroom/sitting room with Eastlake chest and mirror, where you can sit up in bed and survey Bleecker Street, and a den with highriser, shelves of books, a desk, and typewriter. Art work covers all the walls—movie posters, two surprisingly striking vintage Red Cross posters, botanicals. A varied selection of greenery and a colorfully patterned rug add to the charm and warmth.

The hosts are so well liked that guests have been known to throw parties for them before leaving for home. An entry in the guest book reads: "I have a new home in a big city. I will never be lonely again."

GREENWICH VILLAGE. Modern high rise building with views of lower Broadway. Open year-round. Two guest rooms, with a shared bath. Rates: $65 single, $80 double. Continental breakfast included. Children over six welcome; no pets; smoking permitted; MasterCard/Visa/American Express. Close to Chinatown, Little Italy, Washington Square Park, Soho. Two toy poodles in residence. *Represented by Urban Ventures, Inc., New York City.*

NYC—UPPER WEST SIDE

Spacious brownstone in a dynamic area

A sense of spaciousness comes from the fact that this three-story brownstone townhouse is a single-family dwelling. The third floor guest rooms were once the children's bedrooms and retain souvenirs of their adolescence. Just off Columbus Avenue—the most up and coming neighborhood in Manhattan—guests are close to Central Park, the American Museum of Natural History, and Lincoln Center as well as a plethora of fascinating shops and wonderful restaurants.

UPPER WEST SIDE. Brownstone and brick townhouse, built in 1887, with goldfish pond in back yard. Open year-round. Three guest rooms, shared bath. Rates: $45 single, $58 double. Continental breakfast. No children under twelve, no pets; smoking discouraged. Close to Lincoln Center and Columbus Avenue. *Represented by Urban Ventures, Inc., New York City.*

Historical comfort

Between Gramercy and Stuyvesant Parks, in a
old landmark building that traces its history bac
to Peter Stuyvesant, this triplex bed and breakfa
is pure delight. The streets surrounding it ha
been well walked by the famous figures who ha
lived here, such as Mark Twain, O. Henry, Ant
Dvorak, and Samuel Tilden.

Shaded and draped in paisley, the oak floor
parlor has sofas piled high with Persian print
pillows. A Victorian china cupboard, drop le
desk, silver tea service, and an old railroad clo
add interest and warmth. Breakfast is served
a round oak table under a floral crystal d
chandelier.

Whether you are nestled in the bright Mexic
yellow room with pink accents on the lowest le
or two flights up in the space with skyligh
gallery and access to the geranium-potted de
you will be pleased with your surroundings.

The hostess, who is native to Manhattan,
knowledgably direct you, depending upon y
interests. There is a constant blossoming of tre
restaurants in this newly energized area as
as the old standbys like Pete's Tavern,
Anthony's, Fat Tuesdays, and the Gramercy F
Hotel.

GRAMERCY PARK. Landmark brownstone building. Open
round. Two guest rooms with shared bath. Rates: $65 si
$80 double. Expanded continental breakfast included. Chi
welcome; no pets; smoking permitted; MasterCard/Visa/Ame
Express. Near to Gramercy Park, Greenwich Village,
midtown. *Represented by Urban Ventures, Inc., New York*

The common room shared by all the guests.

NYC—CAROLLA DOST B & B

Manhattan's quintessential bed and breakfast

The hostess, a designer of women's clothing, has used the color, style, and decoration elements of her trade, as fine tools. She has transformed two floors of a Murray Hill converted factory building into Manhattan's quintessential bed and breakfast.

Each of the floors has its own living room, dining room, kitchen, and laundry. Six guest rooms with private and shared baths, sleep from one to four people. Ash, peach, honey, and cream hues combine in guest rooms and public spaces. A French display armoire, Oriental carpets, a vintage Japanese screen, and canvas-covered couches are set off by a profusion of healthy greenery. A variety of window exposures frame building tops of Manhattan's famous skyline: Art Deco details, water towers, cartouches that can be glimpsed at dawn's, dusk's, and midnight's revolving light.

The feeling here resembles a European pension. Although the ambiance is casual, guests respect each others privacy. With the freedom to do laundry and to use a country-style kitchen complete with a supply of liquor administered on the honor system, people feel relaxed enough to walk around in their robes. Guests easily come and go, keeping business appointments, sightseeing, discovering New York. Antiques dealers, artists, stock brokers, writers, designers, buyers—Americans and Europeans—find their way here.

Presided over by a beautiful and highly capable hostess, this is a true bed and breakfast in the grand tradition.

CAROLLA DOST. 118 Madison Ave., New York City, NY 10016; (212) 685-4565; Carolla Dost, host. Recently converted office building with splendid views of Manhattan building tops. Open year-round. Six guest rooms, most with private baths. Rates: $85 single, $95 double. $20 each additional person. Children welcome; no pets; smoking permitted; MasterCard/Visa/American Express. Laundry, kitchen, and business facilities including meeting room, secretary, computer, and FAX.

Private decks and modern luxury

East Hampton is a colonial town complete with village green, windmill , and a three-century-old cemetery. Surrounded by gently rolling hills, the area is conducive to quiet activities: walks on the beach, candlelight dinners, reading.

This contemporary cottage is nestled in the treetops, along a quiet lane just outside of town. Its natural siding blends with the landscape, and each room has a private deck and entrance of its own. With the perfect home from which to start the business, these hosts operate the bed and breakfast reservation service, Alternate Lodgings.

EAST HAMPTON . Contemporary home with floor-to-ceiling windows in the living room and a treetop deck. Open April through October. Three guest rooms, private and shared baths. Rates: $65 to $80 double. Continental breakfast daily, often full breakfast on Sunday. No children; no pets; Visa/MasterCard/ American Express. *Represented by Alternate Lodgings, Inc., East Hampton, NY.*

Each luxurious guest room has a private entrance.

Casual elegance on chic Long Island.

Bluejeans and tennis shoes

"If I were asked what to pack for a stay in Amagansett, I would suggest blue jeans and tennis shoes," observes a life-long resident of the area. An artists' enclave for many years, this is one of the quietest of the Hampton's beach communities, though several of the beautiful town beaches do attract a singles crowd.

Along a sandy lane, walking distance to the beach, this home is the casually elegant, year-round residence of two New York City professionals.

AMAGANSETT . New England-style colonial home with private beach. Open year-round. One guest room, private bath. Rates $65 double. Continental or full breakfast available. No children; no pets; smoking discouraged. Within walking distance of the ocean; summer stock, fishing, sailing, excellent dining nearby. *Represented by Alternate Lodgings, Inc., East Hampton, NY.*

PENNSYLVANIA

FAIRWAY FARM

Added attraction: the only trumpet museum in the world

Fairway Farm's claim to fame is its proximity to "the one and only trumpet museum in the world," says Franz Streitwieser, the world-renowned brass musician and historian who founded the museum and opened his house to visitors. Since his children have left home for school, Franz and his wife Katherine have tried to create a European-style bed and breakfast in the tradition of southern Germany and Austria.

The most striking antiques in the household are the Bavarian hand-painted blanket chests dating from 1805 and 1846. A blue-hued bed made in the Black Forest, with a heart-and-floral motif is a bit younger but just as beautiful.

The atmosphere is casual and nonchalant. featuring a wood sauna, spring-fed swimming pool, and asphalt tennis court. Guests are free to roam down to the gazebo or to the pond.

The real fun here, though, is next door. For a suggested donation of $2.50, Franz will take you on a personal tour of the museum, sometimes even unlocking a case to give a musical demonstration. Over four hundred brass instruments fill the cathedral-ceilinged building, including hunting horns, echo instruments, and the world's smallest trumpet. The museum opens up for chamber concerts and lectures, and a musical event is usually scheduled in the gazebo.

Franz and Katherine will also guide visitors to the area's many activities. Ski areas are only forty-five minutes away; the Poconos, one hour. The countryside is rife with antique shops. You might say that a stay at Fairway Farm is a well-orchestrated, harmonious getaway!

FAIRWAY FARM BED AND BREAKFAST, Fairway Farm, Vaughn Rd., Pottstown, PA 19464; (215) 326-1315; Katherine and Franz Streitwieser, hosts. German, French, and Vietnamese spoken. Open September through July. Four guest rooms plus adjoining hallway with Dutch-style foot-to-foot twin beds. Private baths in all except hallway room. Rates: $35, single; $50, double; includes a hearty breakfast with farm-smoked bacon and fresh eggs. Children welcome with supervision; no pets; smoking permitted on terrace; no credit cards.

DIRECTIONS: from the Pennsylvania Turnpike, take exit 23 to Rte. 100 north. Turn right onto Rte. 724 and again onto Vaughan Rd. Follow the signs from there.

Left, a stunning display of trumpets in the museum.

Tiffany windows depict the sea at morning, noon, and night.

HARRY PACKER MANSION

A spectacular wedding present

The age of elegance produced some of the most spectacular architecture of all time. The Harry Packer Mansion is no exception. "An architect used this house as his inspiration for the Haunted Mansion in Walt Disney World," remarked Patricia Handwerk, who, with her husband Bob, is painstakingly restoring the house, keeping the old ceiling paintings, gilt cove work, and other particulars intact wherever possible.

Many of the elaborate, ornate extravagances that characterize the house can be attributed to Asa Packer, the founder of the Lehigh Valley Railroad, who presented the mansion to his son as a wedding present in 1874. From the very outside the noble details begin. Minton tile paves the floor of the Corinthian-columned veranda. The main entrance's 450-pound, etched-glass paneled doors open onto oak parquet floors. The Reception Room, the only common area not furnished according to Packer's plan, sports a walnut mantel and red pine floors. The adjoining library boasts an intricately sculpted mantel of sixteenth-century Caen stone that came from a British manor house. Above the fireplace rests a handsome niche of rich mahogany that follows through into dark paneled walls and a solid-beamed ceiling with oak inserts. The bathroom off the library retains the original mahogany toilet seat, a delicate Limoges basin set in a pink marble sink highlighted by silver spigots. The effect is entrancing.

THE HARRY PACKER MANSION, Packer Hill, Jim Thorpe, PA 18229; (717) 325-8566; Robert and Pat Handwerk, hosts. Some French spoken. Open year round. Second Empire stone-and-brick mansion with cast iron trim. Eight spacious guest rooms, four with private bath. Rates: $65 to $110; carriage house with six rooms, $295; includes a full, elegant breakfast in the dining room. Coffee or breakfast in bed on request. Children are welcome; no pets; smoking in common rooms only. American Express/MasterCard/Visa. Steam train and Victorian high tea on summer weekends, carriage rides on Sundays in warm weather; mule and horseback riding; whitewater canoeing; Lake Mauch Chunk nearby. Call for details concerning Mystery Weekends, balls, and other special events.

DIRECTIONS: from the Pennsylvania Turnpike Northeast Extension, take exit 34. Continue 6 miles south on Rte. 209. Follow signs up the hill to the mansion.

THE CHURCHTOWN INN

Special innkeepers

The Churchtown Inn, a splendid fieldstone mansion, is the most prominent landmark in this tiny village overlooking the pastoral, picture-postcard fields and farms of the Pennsylvania Dutch countryside. Built in 1735, the house was owned by prominent Pennsylvanian Edward Davies, a member of the 25th Congress and a state legislator from 1804 to 1853. It resonates with the solid comforts and grace notes of a home built for gentry. Today, innkeepers Hermine and Stuart Smith and Jim Kent have furnished the house with personal treasures and warm spirits, making for a very relaxed and comfortable inn.

The Smiths' previous life—he was director of the Stuart W. Smith Chorale, which performed in such prestigious houses as Carnegie Hall and Lincoln Center—offered opportunity to globetrot, and this rambling, three-story inn is filled with

The warm and elegant front foyer.

Left, Pennsylvania Dutch countryside viewed from the back patio.

antiques, *objets d'art*, collectibles, and conversation pieces gathered during the Smiths' frequent trips to Europe. In the first-floor parlors you'll find French, English, and American antique furniture, Italian woodcarvings, two hundred Humel figurines, a Regina music box, and Stuart's grand piano. Guest bedrooms are tucked here and there on the second and third floors; antique bedsteads and Amish quilts are the focus of each chamber.

Each Saturday evening guests are offered the rare opportunity to adjourn to a local Amish family's farm to enjoy a bountiful dinner, during which they may be serenaded by the family's five daughters who excel at harmonious religious hymns. Afterward, back at the inn, Stuart often regales his guests with a short piano concert.

THE CHURCHTOWN INN BED BREAKFAST, Rte. 23, Churchtown, PA 17555; mail to P.O. Box 135, RD 3, Narvon, PA 17555; (215) 445-7794; Hermine and Stuart Smith, hosts. Open all year. Eight rooms, 6 with private baths, 2 share. Rates: $45 to $85 double, with full 4 to 5 course breakfast. Children over 12 welcome; no pets; smoking in designated areas; Visa/MasterCard; limited German and Italian spoken. Three-day weekends such as Thanksgiving and Christmas are special, with festive food, decorations, and singing. Area dining includes Pennsylvania Dutch smorgasbord.

DIRECTIONS: going west on Pennsylvania Turnpike take exit 22 (Morgantown) to 23 West for 3 miles to inn. From south take I-83 north to Rte. 30 east to Rte. 23 east.

Above, handmade beds and quilts in the guest rooms. Left, the first-floor breakfast room.

SMITHTON

Pennsylvania Dutch hospitality

In the mid-1700s Henry and Susana Miller were devout members of the Ephrata Community, a Protestant monastic religious group founded by charismatic leader Johann Conrad Beissel. As "outdoor members," the Millers lived by a more relaxed discipline than the majority of disciples, who were celibate and ascetic. The Millers' home, a sturdy stone structure that served as a tavern and stagecoach stop, sat on a hill overlooking the Community Cloister. The Cloister was a remarkably beautiful group of medieval German buildings constructed along the banks of the Cocalico Creek, where Beissel and his followers lived and worked. Although the community of believers declined over the years, the Cloister remains—as does the Millers' home, which is now an inn called Smithton.

Smithton is a warm and welcoming home, and Dorothy Graybill, a Lancaster County native, is the gracious hostess. In this inn guests are steeped in two centuries of history while treated to the the true spirit of Pennsylvania Dutch hospitality. Throughout the house, from the airy kitchen and adjoining dining room to the deluxe, two-story suite complete with Jacuzzi bath, they will enjoy the special attention that is given to wood, from handmade beds and Windsor chairs to hand-fashioned latches and hinges, their design taken from a Cloister pattern. The focal point of each bedroom is the traditional bright and cheerful, handstitched quilt—made by one of the local Mennonite ladies, of course. Extra-large, square down pillows, perfect props for a good read in bed, and soft flannel nightshirts hanging behind each door are just two of many thoughtful and creative touches. Each morning a full breakfast is served by Dorothy, who is assisted by a "plain person," local parlance for the Mennonite and Amish people.

SMITHTON, 900 W. Main St., Ephrata, PA 17522; (717) 733-6094; Dorothy Graybill, hostess. Pennsylvania Dutch spoken. Rustic stone house built in 1762. Five guest rooms plus one suite, all with private baths. Modest extra charge for third person. Open year-round. Rates: $45 to $105 rooms, $130 to $160 for suite, $10 third person (no fee for infants). Full breakfast. Interesting choice of restaurants in area. Children and pets accepted; major credit cards and checks; must prepay in full.

DIRECTIONS: from north or south, take Rte. 222 to the Ephrata exit. Turn west on Rte. 322 (Ephrata's Main Street) and drive 2½ miles to Smithton.

BUCKSVILLE HOUSE

Hospitality and history combined

At the Bucksville House, history and hospitality go hand-in-hand. The inn is a handsome, creamy stucco house and is the most prominent landmark in the tiny village of Bucksville, which lies a stone's throw from the Delaware River and a short drive to the shops and restaurants that line the streets of New Hope.

In 1795 Captain Nicholas Buck built the original building and founded the village of Bucksville. In 1840, Nicholas Buck, Jr. added more rooms and established a stagecoach-stop hotel to serve travelers journeying between Philadelphia and Easton. Innkeepers Barbara and Joe Szollosi are carrying on this tradition of hospitality, and their inn is a little gem.

Guests feel immediately at home, embraced by the warmth of the surroundings. Throughout the inn Barbara and Joe have carefully recreated the colonial era, with additional contemporary comforts, and the house is spotlessly maintained.

In the morning guests gather around the dining room table to enjoy a full breakfast and to revel in the room's rich colonial ambience. During chilly weather the Szollosis stock the hearth with firewood which adds an extra note of cheer. The breakfast menu might include a casserole of savory eggs or eggs and sausages; bran-raisin-walnut waffles; fresh peach fritters, in season; homemade sticky buns or fruit bread; and assorted fresh fruit and hot beverages.

Guest accommodations range in size from the third-floor suite, which boasts exposed beams and a full sitting room, and the second floor Gold Room, which enjoys one of the inn's original hearths, to the intimate Green Room, which contains a winsome display of vintage toys that were Barbara's childhood playthings.

THE BUCKSVILLE HOUSE, RD 2, Box 146, Rte. 412 and Buck Drive, Kintnersville, PA 18930; (215) 847-8948; Barbara and Joe Szollosi, hosts. Open all year. Four rooms and 1 suite share 3 baths. Rates: $45 to $75; suite $120, with full country breakfast and home baking. Children over 12 welcome; no pets; no smoking; Visa/MasterCard, checks accepted. Croquet, horseshoes, walking trails on premises. Fishing, canoeing, swimming, riding, tennis, cross-country skiing, antiquing in area, as well as many restaurants.

DIRECTIONS: from Philadelphia take Rte. 611 North through Doylestown for 14 miles to Rte. 412 North. Take left to inn for 2 miles. From New York take Holland Tunnel to Rte. 78 West to Easton, Pa. to Rte. 611 South through Kintnersville for 1 mile to Church Hill Rd. Take right for 1½ miles to Rte. 412. Inn is second house on left.

This is the heart of Amish country. Although Maple Lane is not an Amish farm—three of its neighbors are—the Rohrers maintain a refreshing air of simplicity and kindness.

MAPLE LANE

In the heart of Amish country

It's Marion Rohrer's touch that makes Maple Lane so special; she adds a homespun air to an otherwise modern colonial home. Pierced parchment lampshades glow into the evenings, when guests curl up in one of Marion's or her daughter-in-law's quilts. Similar coverlets are offered for sale in a nook on the first floor. If the Rohrer family offerings don't fit the bill, Marion kindly directs serious buyers to neighboring Amish farms.

Longtime residents of Paradise, the Rohrers own and operate a working dairy farm with about two hundred head of cows. Ed welcomes guests to watch the milking, and he invites children to help feed the calves. Guests and grandchildren are the Rohrer's hobbies, so Ed loves to answer questions about the farm while Marion keeps track of all the auctions, farmers' markets, and antiques shops.

MAPLE LANE GUEST HOUSE, 505 Paradise Lane, Paradise, PA 17562; (717) 687-7479. Ed and Marion Rohrer, hosts. Open year-round. Four guests rooms with two baths. Modern two-story colonial within sight of a 1785 stone house and Amish farms. Rates: $40 to $50. Includes continental breakfast. Children welcome; no pets; smokers encouraged to use the outside porch in warm weather. Two-night minimum on weekends from April through October. Tourist attractions, shopping, antiquing, historic homes nearby. Pennsylvania Dutch restaurants in abundance.

DIRECTIONS: turn south on Rte. 896 from Rte. 30. Proceed to Strasbourg; turn left on Rte. 896 at the traffic light and continue 1½ miles out of town. Turn right at the sign for the Timberline Lodge. Maple Lane is the first farm on the left.

Cross stitch sampler made by the hostess.

BEECHMONT INN

Breakfast is one of the highlights

Beechmont is a handsome Georgian townhouse, set a few blocks from Hanover's town square and just twenty miles east of historic Gettysburg. Built in 1834, when Andrew Jackson was president, the inn witnessed several major Civil War clashes, first when General Kilpatrick confronted Jeb Stuart and was forced to retreat down the avenue in front of the inn, and again when General George Custer pushed the Confederates back down through the center of Hanover.

Innkeepers Terry and Monna Hormel and Terry's parents Glenn and Maggie furnished their inn with a collection of antiques from the Federal period, befitting the age of the house, as well as a blend of assorted, comfortable period pieces. Two of the inn's three guest suites are located on the first floor. The amply proportioned Diller Suite, with queen-size canopy bed, working fireplace, and equipped kitchenette, is ideal for guests who choose to linger in the area. The Hershey Suite has a private entrance onto the inn's intimate garden courtyard, which is shaded by a century-old magnolia tree. Up the broad and winding central staircase, past a gallery of family portraits, are located the remaining guest rooms— all of which are named after Civil War generals.

The highlight of a stay at Beechmont is breakfast, which is masterfully rendered by chef Terry. House specialties include shirred eggs in bread baskets, a prize-winning homemade granola served with "quark" (a heavenly mix of yogurt, sour cream, sugar, and spices), rice pudding, Hungarian sausage strata, corn custard, and spiced fruit compote.

BEECHMONT INN, 315 Broadway, Hanover, PA 17331; (717) 632-3013; Terry and Monna Hormel, hosts. Open all year. Seven rooms, 3 with private baths, 4 sharing. Rates: $55 to $85 double with full breakfast. Children over 12 welcome; no pets, Visa, MasterCard; smoking in rooms only; French spoken. Fishing, riding, swimming, boating in state park; 3 public golf courses, and many good antique shops in area. Many German country restaurants nearby.

DIRECTIONS: on Rte. 194 on north side of Hanover.

BRAFFERTON INN

Restoration in historic Gettysburg

In 1786, James Getty drew up plans for a new village to rise from the fertile farmlands of southern Pennsylvania. On the first deeded plot was built a sturdy and handsome fieldstone house, designed with deep-set windows, large and rambling rooms, and walls up to two feet thick. As the oldest and most unusual dwelling in all of Gettysburg, the Brafferton Inn witnessed the life and times of this classic American village. The inn (then a private home) was called into duty during the Civil War, serving the community as a church when the local house of worship was pressed into service as a hospital. As battle raged outside the doors of the inn, a bullet found its way into a second-floor mantelpiece, and the wound remains there today.

Happily, today peace reigns supreme under the expert stewardship of owners and innkeepers Jim and Mimi Agard. The Agards spent two years

Hosts Jim and Mimi Agard.

restoring the house, adhering strictly to an eighteenth-century aesthetic, even commissioning well-known folk artist Virginia McLaughlin to paint a striking mural on the four walls of the dining room, depicting the buildings that made up early Gettysburg.

During renovation the Agards purchased the attached house, created a handful of warm, comfortable, and extremely attractive bedrooms, designed a light-filled atrium to connect the two houses, and a fine bed and breakfast inn was born.

Mimi is in command in the kitchen, serving up a hearty, hot breakfast each morning, and she has gained renown for her masterful peaches-and-cream French toast. In fact, so delightful and authentic is every aspect of the historic Brafferton, *Country Living* magazine featured the inn in a lovely article on Gettysburg.

Early Gettysburg is depicted in a mural in the dining room.

THE BRAFFERTON INN, 44–46 York Street, Gettysburg, PA 17325; (717) 337-3423; Mimi and Jim Agard, hosts. Open all year. Eight rooms, 4 with private baths, 4 share. Rates: $65 to $75 double, with full breakfast; $10 extra per child. Children all ages welcome; no pets; Visa/MasterCard; smoking restricted to atrium off dining room. Inn is in center of Gettysburg, within walking distance to restaurants.

DIRECTIONS: right off main traffic circle in downtown.

DULING-KURTZ HOUSE

Creative American fare

If a home with two rooms to let is one end of the bed and breakfast scale, then the Duling-Kurtz House & Country Inn represents the other end. Unlike most inns, this pleasant, clean renovated barn provides such amenities as a telephone and videodisc player in every guest room as well as a heat lamp in a modern bathroom.

The appointments are crisp-looking contemporary reproductions that fit the time and reflect the style of the person for whom each room is named. The light and airy Dolly Madison room with a basket-and-floral paper highlights a white

wicker ensemble. The more sedate Betsy Ross, a room of deep maroon, features primitive country and rattan furniture. The blue-gray and gray color scheme of the James Buchanan room helps to establish a Federal feeling. There are fifteen guest rooms in all, including three suites with sitting area and convertible sofa.

The inn connects via a covered, pillared walkway to a 150 year old stone house with a graceful white enclosed porch on the first floor and open-air veranda on the second. Reserve in advance to eat in one of the seven intimate dining rooms that comprised the original house. Exquisitely prepared entrées include lobster and shrimp Duling-Kurtz, brook trout almondine, Mediterranean shrimp, and grilled breast of pheasant. For special events ask for the *ne plus ultra* Duling-Kurtz Room, which seats two or four in a windowed nook set off from the rest of the dining area with curtains. The $25 rental fee includes a memento of the occasion: silver napkin rings engraved with the celebration's date.

Continental breakfast on a silver tray with the daily paper arrives at your door at a preappointed hour. Freshly squeezed orange juice, croissants, and freshly baked muffins are house specialties.

The inn benefits from its central location—within an hour from Longwood Gardens and Winterthur to the south, Valley Forge National Park to the northeast, and Lancaster County to the west.

DULING-KURTZ HOUSE & COUNTRY INN, South Whitford Rd. Exton, PA 19341; (215) 524-1830; The Pickering Group proprietors. Sally Murray, host. Italian, German, and Arabic spoken. Open all year. Fifteen guest rooms, all with private baths; suites available. Rates: $75 to $120; each additional person, $15; includes continental breakfast in bed. Children welcome; call ahead if traveling with a pet; all major credit cards accepted. Excellent dining in area. Indoor/outdoor tennis, golf and regional attractions.

DIRECTIONS: from Route 30 east continue on through the intersection of Rtes. 100 and 30. The turnoff for the inn is ½ mile west of the junction. Look for the sign.

Ray Constance Hearne making breakfast.

SPRING HOUSE

"Back to basics"

Ray Constance Hearne, a gracious and wise hostess, restored this 1798 family home with a deliberateness guided by a preservationist's philosophy: "Buildings should show their age and reflect their history". Guests wandering through her house see remnant patches of old wall treatments peeking through the whitewash, or, up-stairs, the stenciling that dates back to the 1820s.

When Ray mentions "back to basics," she means antiques, feather beds, down puffs, flannel sheets, and wholesome foods. "I get eggs from chickens that run around outside and eat grass." The tangle of blue and red ribbons that hang by her kitchen window attest to her skills as baker, wine maker, and cook.

The Spring House is a balm for tiredness or frazzled nerves. A weekend here matched with a trip to the nearby Allegro Vineyards, the Susquehanna River, and one of the locale's fine restaurants combines for an excellent cure.

SPRING HOUSE, Muddy Creek Forks, York County, Airville, PA 17302; (717) 927-6906; Ray Constance Hearne, innkeeper. Open year round. Spanish and French spoken. Five guest rooms, two with private baths. Rates: $60 to $85, including a hearty breakfast. Refreshment served on arrival. Children welcome; pets boarded nearby (reservations recommended); no smoking; no credit cards.

DIRECTIONS: from the east take Rte. 202 to the Pennsylvania Turnpike. Pick up Rte. 202 again at King of Prussia (exit Rte. 30 west) and take the Rte. 30 bypass. Go south on 41 to Atglen, 372 west across the Susquehanna, and a right onto 74 north. At Brogue, turn left at the post office. Muddy Creek Forks is 5 miles; at the bottom of the hill is Spring House.

A fascinating collection of paintings decorate the walls.

Roughing it, Philadelphia style.

An original Eames chair in the guest room.

PHILADELPHIA—NORTH

A back-garden greenhouse becomes a fantasy cottage

Decorated with a light and casual hand, this combination greenhouse-and-potting-shed cottage is so inviting that many guests simply disappear for days on end, succumbing to the intimacy of the setting. The cottage shares a broad expanse of lawn with the main house and is bordered on one side by a picturesque grape arbor, and on the other by a large swimming pool. Only twenty-five minutes from Center City, this fantasy cottage is an ideal romantic getaway.

NORTH PHILADELPHIA. Private cottage, a combination greenhouse aod potting shed, on three acres. Open April to September. One guest room (the potting shed), private bath (greenhouse). Rates: $80 one or two people. Continental breakfast can be fixed from ample supplies in refrigerator. No facilities for young children. Swimming pool on premises; stable, tennis, golf nearby. *Represented by Bed & Breakfast of Philadelphia, Philadelphia, PA.*

PHILADELPHIA—NEWMARKET

Federal townhouse near Society Hill

Poised between Society Hill and NewMark visitors to the newly restored areas of "histo Philadelphia" couldn't ask for a more conveni location. Meticulously renovated, this 1811 F eral townhouse beautifully weds mellow wo work, exposed beams and brickwork, a pine flo and working fireplaces with contemporary f nishings. The popular NewMarket shopping dining complex is visible through the Fre doors in the guest bedroom.

NEWMARKET. Federal-style home built in 1810, with con porary décor. Open year-round. Two guest rooms, with pr baths, one with working fireplace. Rates: $60 single, $65 do Hearty continental breakfast; guests may prepare full brea if they wish. No children; no pets. In NewMarket area, w walking distance of the historic district. *Represented by B Breakfast of Philadelphia, Philadelphia, PA.*

PHILADELPHIA—VALLEY FORGE

Well before George Washington

This large stone colonial is an ageless beauty of the pre-Revolutionary period. Nestled on four acres of magnificently wooded land, its title deeds can be traced back to William Penn in 1681.

The original part of the house was built before 1720. Two additions built later create the overall traditional colonial appearance. The last addition was completed in 1791.

Over the years, interior walls have been added and removed, but the original random width plank flooring, with hand-forged nails, remains. The old wood floors, fireplaces, stone walls, and stone smoke house were there when George Washington was at Valley Forge.

A highlight of a stay here is the full English-style breakfast, gracious served in the old part of the house in front of the colonial fireplace with a huge mantel and eight-foot-wide hearth.

Two guest rooms occupy the entire third floor, providing spacious privacy for couples or families. The rose and grey room has a canopied queen-sized bed. The second chamber exudes a fresh "peaches and cream" Victorian look and has an antique double brass bed and a twin bed.

VALLEY FORGE. Open year-round. Three guest rooms, each with a private bath. Rates: $55 single, $65 double. Hearty gourmet full breakfast included. Children welcome; cradle and crib available; guest refrigerator provided; pool in back yard. Five minutes to Valley Forge Park, one-half hour to Philadelphia. *Represented by Bed & Breakfast of Philadelphia, Philadelphia, PA.*

Breakfast is served in the pre-1720 part of the house.

WEDGWOOD INN

Where you can learn all about B & B's

The Wedgwood Inn was built on the foundation of "the old hip roof house" where General Alexander, Lord Stirling, stayed during the Revolutionary War. It is therefore fitting that the inn was recently designated to participate in New Hope's celebration of Washington's crossing the Delaware.

Situated two miles from that site, the inn is just four blocks from the center of New Hope. Named after Josiah Wedgwood, many of the inn's rooms have a blue and white theme. An ever-growing collection of Wedgwood porcelain is scattered throughout the house and a whatnot in the parlor displays among other things, a tea set from Queen Elizabeth's coronation, Jasper ware, and a commemorative bicentennial piece.

Guest rooms are comfortably furnished with period pieces. Cubist and Abstract paintings by Nadine's great-aunt combine favorably with a collection of contemporary crafts pieces to create an interesting effect.

In addition to running the inn, Carl and Nadine offer prospective innkeepers week-long seminars in running an inn or bed and breakfast. Everything is covered, from locating and financing a place to checking in guests, and candidates are given an opportunity to test the waters.

Extras at the Wedgwood include breakfast in bed, an afternoon fireside tea, Carl's homemade almond liqueur, and a complimentary ride into town in a Pennsylvania Dutch horse-drawn buggy.

WEDGWOOD INN, 111 West Bridge Street, New Hope, PA 18938; (215) 862-2570; Carl Glassman and Nadine Silnutzer, hosts. Open year-round. Twelve guest rooms including two suites, most with private baths; carriage house with private bath, deck, and kitchenette. Rates: $60-$95 for room with private bath. Inquire for rates on suites and carriage house. Children accepted, call in advance; pets permitted, call in advance; no smoking; personal checks, travelers checks, cash. Two blocks from center of New Hope.

DIRECTIONS: from I-95 take the New Hope exit and proceed north 10 miles to the center of town. Turn left at the traffic light (only one in town) and continue up hill for 3 blocks. Wedgwood is at top of hill on left.

BARLEY SHEAF FARM

Romance and charm for blithe spirits

A sense that all's right with the world is the hallmark of the best inns. Barley Sheaf Farm in Bucks County emanates that wonderful feeling of security and comfort.

The property has attracted blithe and sophisticated spirits throughout its life, most notably when it was owned by playwright George S. Kaufman, and weekend guests included Moss Hart, Lillian Hellman, S.J. Perlman, and Alexander Woollcott.

Today, Ann and Don Mills' guests may stay in the farmhouse or in one of three bedrooms in the converted ice house. Bedrooms in the main house vary in size, but total charm is assured in each. A two-room suite furnished with an impressive brass sleigh bed, broad and comfortable upholstered couch, working fireplace, and French doors with handpainted privacy screen is the largest bedchamber. The separate ice house, comprising a living room with three very individual, country-style bedrooms, is tailor-made for couples traveling together.

A great percentage of the foodstuffs for a truly splendid breakfast come from the farm; the Millses raise chickens, keep bees, and harvest a large crop of raspberries each year. A puffy soufflé made from fresh eggs, buttery biscuits dripping with Barley Sheaf honey, feather-light pancakes and fresh raspberry sauce garnished with nutmeg-flecked sour cream, a homemade sausage ring, apple crêpes filled with cheese, nuts, and raisins and napped with homemade apple syrup, a sour cream coffee cake—need one say more to describe total satisfaction?

BARLEY SHEAF FARM, Box 10, Rte. 202, Holicong, PA 18928; (215) 794-5104; Ann and Don Mills, and Don Mills, Jr., hosts. French spoken by Ann. Open February 14 through last weekend before Christmas; weekends only January to February 14. Six guest rooms in main house, plus three in cottage; private baths. Rates: $95 to $135, $15 per extra person. Full breakfast served. Wide selection of restaurants in area. No children under eight; no pets; checks accepted.

DIRECTIONS: from Philadelphia, take I-95 north to exit 332 (Newtown). Turn left at exit and drive to third light, turning right onto Rte. 532. Take first left at Goodnoes Restaurant and then turn right onto Rte. 413 north. Follow 413 for about twelve minutes and turn right at intersection of Rte. 202. Farm is on the right about a five-minute drive on 202.

THE WHITEHALL INN

A handsome estate n Bucks County

Bucks County is blessed with lush countryside lled with handsome estates that have sheltered enerations of landed gentry. And no Bucks County estate is more lovely than the Whitehall nn. The inn sits secluded on a quiet country yway, yet it is nearby the center of bustling New Iope.

Mike and Suella Wass are the innkeepers xtraordinaire of this 1795 great house, and their ision of hospitality would exhaust lesser mortals. A day at the Whitehall begins with a leisurely our-course breakfast, prepared by Suella and erved by Mike. The Wasses' litany of gourmet reakfast fare is longer than your arm, fit for a our-star restaurant, and striking enough to be eatured by *Bon Appetit* magazine. The meal is erved on fine European china and crystal, but he real treasure is the Wasses' rare, heirloom terling, passed down through Suella's family, vhich is placed, in proper English fashion, top-

eft above, the elegant breakfast table set with heirloom ilver.

side-down to reveal the intricacies of the design on the backs.

These energetic innkeepers don't stop here. Mike makes his own bath salts, as well as fragrant rose-scented potpourri, concocted from petals gathered from his prized rose collection; and the Wasses attend to such details as providing each guest room with lead crystal wine glasses and a full bottle of wine produced by a Bucks County vineyard. Each day they prepare a sweet and savory afternoon tea, and they periodically host a theme tea, whose topic pervades the entire weekend. For example: a candlelight tea accompanied by Philadelphia's Fairmount Brass Quartet or by a trio from the New York Philharmonic; a strawberry tea or a chocolate tea, each attended by a speaker knowledgeable on the subject; a romantic champagne-and-candlelight New Year's Eve classical music concert.

THE WHITEHALL INN, RD 2, Box 250, 1370 Pineville Rd., New Hope, PA 18938; (215) 598-7945; Mike and Suella Wass, hosts. Open all year. Six rooms, 4 with private baths, 2 share. $85 to $125 double, with full candlelit breakfast and afternoon high tea. Children over 12 welcome; no pets; no smoking; all major credit cards accepted. Swimming pool and tennis courts on premises, and dressage horses that accept carrots from guests. All of Bucks County's famous attractions immediately available, including restaurants, menus of which are available at inn.

DIRECTIONS: from New Hope on Rte. 202 go to traffic light at Street Rd. intersection. Turn left on Street to 2nd intersection at Pineville Rd. Turn right for 1½ miles to inn.

Each of the spacious guest rooms is furnished in a different period.

PINEAPPLE HILL

The symbol of hospitality

The streets of New Hope are thickly lined with chic shops and restaurants that cater to the great flow of tourists visiting Bucks County each year. This bustling village is the county's hub. Just four miles from New Hope's commercial center, Pineapple Hill offers the intimacy and comfort of a family home with the convenience of the town's close proximity.

In colonial times, the pineapple symbolized hospitality. True to its name, Pineapple Hill offers travelers comfort and friendly intimacy in an authentic colonial setting.

The hosts, Randy and Suzie Leslie, have decorated their home with American country furnishings, mostly from Pennsylvania and Virginia: antique quilts, coverlets and crocks, folk and primitive art. Suzie's superb collection of antique spools is displayed throughout the house.

The house was built in several sections, and five antique-filled guest rooms are thus divided, three in two second-floor wings and two under the third-floor eaves. Two separate suites are perfect for families or for two couples.

One of the most striking features of Pineapple Hill is its backyard stone ruins. Where a colonial barn once stood, there is a swimming pool made private and scenic by the barn's preserved foundations.

The grounds are ideal for walking, jogging, and, in winter, cross-country skiing. The Delaware Canal towpath borders the grounds and invites canoers and rafters.

PINEAPPLE HILL, 1324 River Road, New Hope, PA 18938; (215) 862-9608; Randy and Suzie Leslie, hosts. Open year-round. Five guest rooms including two suites, three with private baths. Rates: $55-$95, including generous continental breakfast. Snacks and beverages always available. Children during week; no pets; no smoking; American Express, checks accepted. Swimming pool on premises, excellent dining in area.

DIRECTIONS: from Philadelphia, take I-95 to New Hope/Yardley exit. Drive north on Taylorsville Rd. to junction with Rte. 32. Inn is 100 yards north on 32, second driveway on right. From New York City, take New Jersey Tpke. south to exit 10. Take I-287 north to Rte. 22 and 22 west to Rte. 202. Take 202 south to New Hope exit (first in Penn.). Drive south through New Hope on River Rd. (Rte. 32). Continue 4.6 miles beyond traffic light. Inn is on left across from Thorpe Farm sign.

BRIDGETON HOUSE

French doors onto the Delaware

Bridgeton House sits on the banks of the Delaware River. This is an enviable position, for while many Bucks County hostels advertise proximity to the river as a drawing card, few can truly say the river is their backyard. Beatrice and Charles Briggs restored their seven-room inn with an eye to incorporating the river by installing French doors and laying a pebble patio that sweeps to the edge of the riverbank.

With Charles' talent as a master carpenter and Bea in charge of interior design, the Briggses completely renovated and decorated what was a derelict building, an eyesore caught between the bridge and the road. Today, Bridgeton House feels like a cross between American country-naive and French provincial style. Bea uses soft color throughout, Williamsburg shades of faded cobalt, muted mulberry, and clotted cream. Thick rag rugs and a collection of antique Oriental area rugs accent painted hardwood floors. Fine bed linens and puffy comforters please the eye and assure the traveler of a comfortable night's sleep.

Bridgeton House is a casual, but sophisticated environment. Before becoming innkeepers, Bea and Charles worked in Bucks County inns and restaurants, and their years of experience show. Always available, but never intrusive, Bea sets a relaxing tone. She loves to cook and often can be found in the inn's beautiful kitchen, which opens onto the entry hall and adjoining dining room.

Outside the door, the Delaware River affords many diversions, starting with its lovely sixty-mile towpath, which is perfect for hiking, cross-country skiing, picnicking, and jogging. Canoeing, fishing, and tubing enthusiasts proclaim the Delaware to be among the East Coast's finest rivers.

BRIDGETON HOUSE, River Rd., Upper Black Eddy, PA 18972; (215) 982-5856; Charles and Beatrice Briggs, proprietors. Built in 1836 as a private residence, this home also once served as a bakery and candy store. Open year-round. Seven guest rooms, four with river views and balconies, all with private baths. Rates: on weekends by room $85–$95, during week $85 per room. Full breakfast. Good restaurants close by. Children discouraged; no pets; no smoking; personal checks accepted. Swimming, tubing on Delaware River, tow path, fishing, biking, antiques.

DIRECTIONS: from Philadelphia, take I-95 north to New Hope/Yardley exit. Follow signs north to New Hope. Continue north on Rte. 32, 18 miles to inn.

The elegant entry hall.

THE INN AT FORDHOOK FARM

Burpee seeds branches out

The Inn at Fordhook Farm stands as a monument to quiet, old world elegance. Three generations of the Burpee family, purveyors of world-class seeds, entertained guests in this charming, predominantly eighteenth-century fieldstone residence. The tradition is continuing since Blanche Burpee Dohan and Jonathan Burpee, the firm's founder's grandchildren, opened the house as an eminently comfortable bed and breakfast.

Each of the five rooms, named for different family members, has its own appeal, although honeymoon couples tend to gravitate to the spacious Burpee Room with its colonial revival fireplace and private balcony or to the stately Atlee Room, accented with leaded glass windows, fireplace, and balcony. The smaller Curtiss Room is a cozy nook with slanted roof and gorgeous view of the grounds. Double pocket doors distinguish the Torrance Room, as sunshine, peach hues, and three mirrored closet panels enhance the Simmons Room. The linden tree outside is a "a favorite haunt of the hoot owl," says Blanche.

Trees form an outstanding backdrop here along with the numerous gardens, including former seed-trial beds. Daffodils carpet the lawn's edge in spring, while marigolds last until the first frost. Lilacs, wisteria, and perennials dot the grounds amid gingkos, sycamores, dogwood, magnolia, rhododendrons and azalea, all befitting the gracious home of one of the most famous men in seed history.

THE INN AT FORDHOOK FARM, 105 New Britain Rd., Doylestown, PA 18901; (215) 345-1766; Blanche Burpee Dohan and Laurel Raymond, innkeepers. Open all year. French and German spoken. Five guest rooms, 3 with private baths, 2 with fireplaces; suite arrangement available. Rates: $72 to $98; additional person, $17; 2-bedroom carriage house from $125 to $164. Full farm breakfast included; afternoon tea served on the terrace. Children over 12 welcome; no pets; smoking on the terrace only; Visa/MasterCard/American Express. Tubing, canoeing, rafting, swimming, tennis, horseback riding, ice skating, cross-country skiing; Mercer Museum and Moravian Tile Works; antiquing. Excellent dining in the area.

DIRECTIONS: The Inn at Fordhook Farm is located at Rte. 202 and the 611 bypass, 1.6 miles west of Doylestown. From Doylestown follow Rte. 202 south past the hospital and over the 611 bypass. Turn left on New Britain Rd. (first road on your left next to Delaware Valley College). The entrance to Fordhook is ¼ mile on your left through two stone pillars. Follow the drive over the little bridge to the large stone house on the right.

Left, the grand house and sweeping lawns. Above, the Breakfast Room.

Left, the rear garden and house. Above, a very private top-floor guest room.

SWEETWATER FARM

A fieldstone mansion

The setting is the Brandywine Valley, inspiration to generations of American artists. The inn is a Georgian manor house, a superb fieldstone mansion dating to 1758.

Sweetwater Farm sits at the end of a deep, circular drive, completely secluded on fifteen acres of field and forest. Its stately lines are complemented by towering shade trees and thoughtfully landscaped gardens. The house has played its part in American history, sheltering war-weary Revolutionary War soldiers, hosting the Marquis de Lafayette, and hiding slaves as they traveled the perilous Underground Railway. Innkeeper Linda Kaat, the steward of this romantic and peaceful hideaway, is singleminded in her pursuit of excellence. She has furnished the formal parlors of the inn with a trove of eighteenth and nineteenth-century antiques and filled the open kitchen and rustic mudroom with wonderful primitive pieces, antique yellow ware, and fragrant garden herbs drying in decorative bunches.

Guest accommodations are found on the second and third floors of the main house and in several detached cottages. Each bedroom is completely comfortable, immaculate, and thoughtfully decorated, and the two located at the top of the house are particularly private and spacious.

Each morning guests are served an ample country breakfast which features eggs gathered fresh from the inn's free-range chickens. During summer months the inn's swimming pool or broad rear veranda, which overlooks the pool and surrounding fields and gardens, beckon. From this vantage point one can savor the delicious feeling of calm that pervades this sweet oasis.

SWEETWATER FARM, Sweetwater Road, Glen Mills, PA 19342; (215) 459-4711; Linda Kaat, host. Open all year. Twelve rooms with private baths. Rates: $125 to $250 double, with full country breakfast. Children welcome, although inn is not child-proof; pets accepted with discretion; Visa/MasterCard/American Express accepted. This is a working horse and sheep farm, and there is a swimming pool on the premises. Being situated in the famous Brandywine Valley, such attractions as Winterthur and Longwood Gardens are memorable. There are various historic taverns, inns, and restaurants in the area for dining.

DIRECTIONS: from north on New Jersey Turnpike take exit 2 onto Rte. 322 West into Pa. and exit at Rte. 452 North. After 4½ miles go left on Rte. 1 for 1 mile to Valley Rd. at the Franklin Mint intersection. Take right for 1½ miles to T junction and left and immediate right for ¾ miles to Sweetwater Rd. Left for ½ mile to farm on left.

NEW JERSEY

CHESTNUT HILL ON THE DELAWARE

Old-fashioned and very romantic

Visitors to Linda and Rob Castagna's home, Chestnut Hill, are enveloped by the warmth of the atmosphere and the beauty of the setting on the banks of the Delaware.

Bedrooms are old-fashioned and very romantic, thanks to Linda's gift for color and design and her many small touches. On the door of each room hangs a delicate wreath, and inside a handcrafted cloth basket is filled with fresh fruit in season. One room, entitled Peaches and Cream, is an aptly named chamber with soft peach-striped wallpaper, puffy peach comforter draped with a lace coverlet, and an oak chest of drawers and armoire. The Pineapple Room, which was the servants quarters, is roomy and private at the rear of the second floor. Decorated in cream, yellows,

and greens, the room offers a bed dressed with a luxurious Welsh duvet and a wall of built-in drawers and cabinets in which hides a television. Bayberry features a bay window fitted with original shutters and is decorated in sprightly primary shades taken from colors in the bed's antique quilt.

Up a steep staircase to the attic suite, the bridal favorite, guests are in a world of their own. One bedroom is named Teddy's Place and contains several furry bears and a Little Golden Book of the *Three Bears* tale. Against a warm and rosy red print wallpaper, white eyelet and ruffled bedclothes look crisp and inviting. The bathroom, which displays beautiful Italian tile work, overlooks the swift-flowing Delaware.

CHESTNUT HILL ON THE DELAWARE, 63 Church St., Milford, NJ 08848; (201) 995-9761; Linda and Rob Castagna, hosts. Victorian house built in 1860, with gallery/gift shop on premises. Open year-round. Five guest rooms, shared and private baths. Rates: $60 to $85, $120 suite. Full breakfast served. Excellent dining in area. No pets; no smoking; checks accepted.

DIRECTIONS: from Milford, turn right at light and right again on Church St. (1 street before Delaware River bridge). Turn left into dead-end, which is Chestnut Hill's parking area.

Left, a photograph of the hosts and their son, dressed in the period clothes that they love to collect.

THE OLD HUNTERDON HOUSE

A guest list of celebrities

Directly across the Delaware River from Bucks County, amidst wooded hills and rolling farmlands, lies the village of Frenchtown, abounding in fine restaurants, galleries, and quaint antiques shops. Comfort awaits the traveler at The Old Hunterdon House, a striking old mansion built at the time of the Civil War.

After acquiring the house a few years ago and restoring it to its former grandeur, Rick Carson scoured the countryside seeking authentic period furniture to enrich it. Ornate Victorian and Empire pieces, burled wood bedsteads, dazzling chandeliers, and oriental rugs on wide-planked floors all meld harmoniously.

The house was formerly the residence of the Apgar family, owners of the nearby National Hotel. Guests spilled over to the Apgars' residence when the hotel was full. That's how Annie Oakley, William White, and other notables happened to sleep here.

THE OLD HUNTERDON HOUSE, 12 Bridge Street, Frenchtown, NJ 08825; (201) 996-3632; Rick Carson, innkeeper. Open year round. Seven distinctive guest rooms, all with private baths. Rates: $65 to $90; special single rate Monday thru Thursday; two night stay required if stay includes Saturday. Includes continental breakfast. No young children; no pets; smoking permitted. MasterCard/Visa.

DIRECTIONS: from New York City take New Jersey Turnpike to I-78. Go west to exit 15. Turn left onto Route 513 to Pittstown. Continue on 513 to Frenchtown. Inn is on main street, ½ block from river. From Philadelphia take I-95 north across bridge into New Jersey. Take 1st exit (New Jersey Route 29) north into Frenchtown.

PHOTOGRAPHS BY BILL BAKER

The Victorian furnishings reflect the Civil War vintage of the house.

JERICA HILL

Restored to match childhood memories

When Judith Studer was a child growing up in Flemington, New Jersey, she visited this old Victorian home that belonged to her best friend's grandfather.

It had been built by a local businessman who owned a neighboring lumberyard, and no effort had been spared in fitting the generously proportioned rooms with the finest woods. Five years ago she bought it, by then in a state of total disrepair. Lovingly she has restored it to match her wonderful childhood memories of gleaming hardwood floors and finely polished intricate woodwork. The exterior has been painted to reflect her own vibrant vision of Jerica Hill—a vivid gray with burgundy shutters and soft pearl gray trim.

The guest rooms have been named after Judith's relatives who lived in the area. Period pieces adorn each of the distinctive rooms: wicker and brass, oak, antique pine, and formal mahogony furniture. Antique spreads, coverlets, and country quilts dress up the beds. Lots of family pieces and things gathered up from the area appear throughout. Each guest room is supplied with fresh flowers, fruit, and sparkling water.

Born into the hostelry business, Judith grew up with parents who owned Flemington's historic Union Hotel, across the street from where the Lindbergh trial was held in the 1930's. For more than four generations her family has lived and worked in the area.

If you were born to shop, the town is awash with better than eighty outlets including Flemington Furs, Calvin Klein, Villeroy & Boch, and Waterford crystal. Many are within walking distance. When you are tired of shopping, Judith can arrange for a Champagne hot air balloon flight or picnic tours of the wineries in the beautiful Delaware River Valley.

JERICA HILL, 96 Broad Street, Flemington, NJ 08822; (201) 782-8234; Judith S. Studer, innkeeper. Open all year. Five guest rooms with private and shared baths. Rates: $55 to $80 double. Includes expanded continental breakfast. Children over twelve welcome; no pets; no smoking; Visa/MasterCard/American Express. Two cats on premises. Hot air balloon flights and winery tours of Delaware River Valley arranged here. Outlet shopping galore in Flemington's "Liberty Village".

DIRECTIONS: from U.S. 202 traveling north or south proceed to U.S. 202/Rte. 31 traffic circle to Rte. 31 north off circle. At first traffic light turn left onto Church St. and proceed 2 blocks to Broad St. Turn right and continue 2 blocks to 96 Broad St.

The largest, most imposing guest room.

THE NORMANDY INN

Gracious privacy a block from the beach

Of all the seaside villages that attract vacationers to the New Jersey shore, none is more gracious than Spring Lake. Bypassed by the teeming hordes who populate streets, casinos, and beaches of larger resorts, Spring Lake emanates a special grace particular to communities made up of broad avenues lined with grand, tree-shaded "cottages."

Built in 1888 as a private residence and expanded in 1916, The Normandy Inn, which comprises twenty bedrooms, sits one block from the beach. Size alone makes the Normandy feel like a small resort hotel, though innkeepers Susan and Michael Ingino, who live in the house year-round with daughter Beth, maintain a warm and homey atmosphere.

Breakfast at this inn is especially generous and delicious. Each morning guests seat themselves in the large dining room—a room of such scale that young Beth dreams of converting it into her own private skating rink. The written menu offers many choices. Besides the requisite juices, hot beverages, and cold cereals, the Inginos serve real Irish porridge, four types of pancakes, two sorts of French toast, six varieties of eggs, four breakfast meats, and Michael's fresh-baked muffins or soda bread. Breakfast is Michael's favorite meal, and as a chef, he sees to it that guests need eat but a sparing lunch.

The Inginos are avid collectors of Victoriana and have almost completed furnishing each room with antiques and details from the period. Rooms vary in size, but each is clean and very comfortable.

THE NORMANDY INN, 21 Tuttle Ave., Spring Lake, NJ 07762; (201) 449-7172; Michael and Susan Ingino, hosts. Italianate Victorian home near beach offers casual comfort and thoughtful amenities. Open all year. Eighteen guest rooms in house, two over garage, most with private baths. Rates $86 to $115 in season, $70 to $90 off season, double occupancy. Includes full breakfast. Good dining throughout area. Children who enjoy quietude welcome; no pets; smoking discouraged; American Express. Area offers beach, horseback riding, antiques.

DIRECTIONS: from north, take Garden State Pkwy. to exit 98 (Rte. 34). Proceed south on 34 to traffic circle. Drive ¾ way around and turn right on Rte. 524 east. Cross Rtes. 35 and 71. Rte. 524 then becomes Ludlow Ave. Proceed to end of Ludlow and turn right onto Ocean Ave., then first right onto Tuttle. From south, take Garden State Pkwy. to exit 98 (Rte. 38 E). Cross Rte. 18 and turn right at next traffic light onto New Bedford Rd. Take sharp left at second stop sign (Rte. 524) and proceed as above.

CONOVER'S BAY HEAD INN

The pearl of seaside inns

Beverly Conover's light touch and delicate sense of color reveal an exquisite aesthetic sensitivity that defines the inn—from the embracing warm tones of lavender and mauve on the first floor to the family photographs she has framed and placed in each room.

Every one of the twelve dignified bedrooms has a distinct personality. The brightest room is also the most dramatic. Splashes of red and green in the geranium wallpaper match the brilliant red of the table skirt and ruffled cushion on the white wicker settee. In another room, a smoke-blue and white Laura Ashley print on the wall is reversed on the chair upholstery. In yet another, a spool bed and curly maple dresser are paired with pink and lime linens, a green stenciled border, and a row of small porcelain ducks that nest on top of the window sill.

The views are equally impressive. The sinuously curved maple bed in one third-floor room is placed so that reclining guests can see the bay, marina, and yacht club. Reflections of the ocean gleam in other rooms. Shapely old-style shingle houses comprise the rest of the scenic landscape.

Bay Head captures the feel of a late nineteenth-century residential summer village. The few, quaint shops sell antiques, art wear, prints, books, gifts, and clothing. Very little tells of life's more pressing necessities. "Which is as it should be," notes Beverly.

"I like to fuss. I always fuss over breakfast," Beverly adds. Inspired baked goods grace the table as beautifully as the place settings. Fresh-squeezed orange juice and cut fruit appear on the table every day, and on Sunday Beverly prepares a tasty egg dish. Guests can dine in the sunny breakfast room, on the manicured lawn, or on the front porch.

Conover's is a classic among bed and breakfasts, the pearl of seaside inns.

CONOVER'S BAY HEAD INN, 646 Main Ave., Bay Head, NJ 08742; (201) 892-4664; Carl and Beverly Conover, hosts. Open February 15 to December 15. Summer cottage built in 1912 and located one block from the beach. Twelve guest rooms; six second-story guest rooms have private baths; six third-story rooms share two baths. Rates: $65 to $100 in season; off-season discounts; $20 for additional person; singles $5 to $10 less double rate. Light breakfast included. Tea served in the afternoons until May 1. Children aged 13 and up are welcome in July and August only; no pets; outdoor smoking; American Express/MasterCard/Visa. Lawn games; golf; tennis; winter sports on Twilight Lake; beach; windsurfing.

DIRECTIONS: from the Garden State Parkway, take Rte. 34 (exit 98) and follow signs for Rte. 35. Continue on Rte. 35 south into Bay Head. The inn is on the right.

Some of John Peto's paintings, including a self-portrait on the easel.

THE STUDIO OF JOHN F. PETO

A secluded artist's studio

Gifted in the art of still life, John F. Peto, who lived during the latter half of the nineteenth century, was an artist whose talent was to go unrecognized in his lifetime. Throughout his career, he was unfavorably compared to friend and fellow painter William Michael Harnett. In 1950 the tide began to turn when the Brooklyn Museum mounted Peto's first major exhibition. Thirty-three years later when the National Gallery of Art organized a retrospective that traveled from Washington, D.C. to the Amon Carter Museum in Fort Worth, Texas, Peto finally emerged as a major American painter, now considered by many to be a far greater talent than Harnett.

Peto lived his life in virtual seclusion in Island Heights, a quiet village along the New Jersey shore, in a house he built overlooking the Tom's River. He first designed a studio for himself, a spacious and high-ceilinged room with white stuccoed fireplace, white walls, and "Peto red" wainscoting. He then built his home, including seven bedrooms, around the studio.

Granddaughter Joy Peto Smiley, as ebullient as her forebears were reclusive, has opened her grandfather's home and studio to overnight guests. Rooms are furnished much as they always have been, unpretentious with an eclectic mix of beds, chest, and chairs. In the common rooms hang reproductions of Peto's most famous paintings, and the studio holds a small selection of his original works.

Whether dining on Joy's "ethereal eggs," fresh fruit, and hot popovers, or walking through historic Island Heights, the studio, filled with the strong and quiet presence of John Peto, is the most memorable part of a stay.

THE STUDIO OF JOHN F. PETO, 102 Cedar Ave., Island Heights, NJ 08732; (201) 270-6058; Joy Peto Smiley, hostess. Open year-round. Seven guest rooms, shared baths. Rates: $45 to $65. Hearty breakfast served. Variety of restaurants, including a wonderful seafood eatery, in the area. Children twelve and over; no pets; American Express, personal checks.

DIRECTIONS: take Garden State Pkwy. to exit 82 east. Pass through six stoplights. Two blocks further, turn right onto Central Ave. and drive ¼ mile; halfway up the first hill, turn left onto Summit. Drive 4 blocks and turn right onto Cedar. Inn is 2 blocks on left (look for sign "The Studio").

MANOR HOUSE INN

Engaging innkeepers in Cape May

Cape May's Hughes Street is lined with gracious homes and lush shade trees, and it is one of the choicest addresses in the village. To make matters complete, the street is centrally located, between the shops and restaurants of the pedestrian mall, and the ocean beach.

One of the most relaxed and engaging places to stay along this tranquil byway is the Manor House, ably operated by Tom and Mary Snyder. Juxtaposed with the gingerbread opulence of many nearby inns, the Manor House is comparatively modest and unassuming. This inn is a spacious, three-story Colonial Revival home, iced with weathered shingles, capped with a gambrel roof, and girded in front by an old-fashioned "sitting" porch—a favorite hang-out during the balmy days of summer. Inside, everything is spit-and-polish perfection, *sans* even an iota of ostentation. The

entry hall, with its gleaming oak staircase, chestnut wainscoting, and subtly-shaded, stained glass windows, bespeaks the overall quality of the house.

Growing up among the hearty eaters of the Pennsylvania Dutch country, Mary combines heritage and experience to serve up substantial fare that satisfies the contemporary palate. A sampling includes a delectable apple-cheese pancake; eggs baked with Canadian bacon, Swiss cheese, and sour cream; and sticky buns made with a yeasty potato dough.

The Manor House is gaining renown—or, in some quarters, notoriety—for the brand of humor Tom dishes out each morning. Dressed like a Victorian gentleman in starched dress shirt, bow tie, and braces, he regales his guests with extemporaneous renditions of "What's Happening Now In Cape May." Though he's considered by many to be Cape May's answer to Garrison Keillor, Tom is quick to point out that there's more than a smattering of Henny Youngman humor in his delivery.

Each bedroom is brightened by a beautiful quilt, many of which were created by host Mary Snyder.

MANOR HOUSE INN, 612 Hughes Street, Cape May, NJ 08204; (609) 884-4710; Mary and Tom Snyder, hosts. Open Feb. 1 to Dec. 31. Ten rooms, 4 with private baths and 6 sharing 3½ baths. Rates: $60 to $120. Children over 12 welcome; no pets; major credit cards accepted; Pensylvania Dutch spoken. Traditional seafood and "creative cuisine" restaurants in area.

DIRECTIONS: from bridge into Cape May follow Lafayette St. for 8 blocks to Franklin and turn left for 2 blocks to Hughes. Turn right. If street parking is full, pull into driveway next to sign.

Left, one of two opulent dining rooms, where breakfast is served in courses.

COLUMNS BY-THE-SEA

Salty seabreezes and sounds of the surf

The sound of the surf lapping a sandy beach and the heady scent of a salty seabreeze lull guests at the Columns By The Sea. This grand inn is one of the few bed and breakfast establishments in historic Cape May to rest on the water's edge, along a quiet stretch of private homes well removed from the bustling esplanade.

The exterior is an eclectic mix of styles pulled together by a commodious, columned veranda which faces the ocean. Entering the mansion, one is enveloped by its Victorian past, thanks to innkeepers Barry and Cathy Rein. When they fell in love with this grand relic of the gilded age they embarked on a thorough restoration, and the result is this authentically furnished inn.

One of the highlights of the first-floor parlor, which boasts a handcarved coffered ceiling and beautifully paneled staircase, is a collection of exquisite antique Chinese ivory carvings. Two dining rooms adjoin the parlor and they display a treasure trove of antique china and 19th-century prints and paintings.

Each morning guests adjourn to these rooms to enjoy a gourmet breakfast served on massive dining tables draped with linen and antique lace. Breakfast begins with fresh fruit and moves on to a hot entrée such as "decadent" French toast, spinach soufflé, or asparagus strata. Champagne accompanies the inn's Sunday meal, which often features a delectable cheese blintz soufflé. Besides breakfast, guests are offered an afternoon tea which might include the Reins' trademark iced coffee (made with both cream *and* ice cream) and such appetizing morsels as Chinese egg rolls or Mexican tostadas. To top off the day, an evening tot of sherry or port is accompanied by a home-baked sweet.

COLUMNS BY-THE-SEA, 1513 Beach Drive, Cape May, NJ 08204; (609) 884-2228; Barry and Cathy Rein, hosts. Open April to Oct. Eleven rooms with private baths. Rates: $95 to $125 double, with gourmet breakfast, afternoon tea, and evening treats; Champagne Sunday brunch. Children over 12 welcome; no pets; no credit cards; German spoken. Dolphin watching from inn plus all of Cape May's recreational activities. Ten minutes drive to Italian, Cajun, Mexican, continental, and seafood dining.

DIRECTIONS: at southern end of Garden State Parkway to Cape May, follow signs to beach and turn left at Beach Drive. Inn is between Baltimore and Brooklyn streets.

with the guests; music played on an antique harp or an 1850 square grand piano in the parlor, which functions essentially as a music room; all these add to the atmosphere of life in another time—less hurried, less hectic, less harrowing.

Cape May is the nation's oldest seaside resort, and a stroll along its tree-lined, gaslit streets at dusk on a summer's evening recreates the heyday of the nineteenth century: ice cream parlors, Sousa brass bands, bicycles, carriages, knickered boys, hoops, and the backdrop to it all, the incredible collection of hundreds of extravagantly ornamented Victorian houses built in Italianate and Gothic Revival styles, among which The Abbey stands out.

THE ABBEY, Columbia Avenue and Gurney Street, Cape May, NJ 08204; (609) 884-4506; Jay and Marianne Schatz, hosts. Open April through November. Fourteen rooms, eleven with private baths in two adjacent houses. Rates: $58 to $110 per couple; includes full breakfast in spring and fall, lighter buffet in summer, and afternoon refreshments through the year, and on-site parking for main house. No liquor served; guests may bring their own. Well-behaved children over 12 welcome; no pets; all smoking limited to the veranda; Visa/MasterCard/American Express. Croquet at the inn, seashore swimming one block away, and many other activities.

DIRECTIONS: in Cape May, turn left on Ocean street, drive 3 blocks and turn left on Columbia Avenue. The inn is one block down.

THE ABBEY

Casual elegance

One of the more elaborate carpenter gothic houses in Cape May is a seaside villa built in 1869 by a wealthy coal baron who spared no expense in creating an architectural masterpiece for entertaining summer guests at the sea shore. Now transformed into a bed and breakfast of expansive proportions by Jay and Marianne Schatz, the building has been delightfully restored. The interior contains a variety of decorative Victorian wallpaper reproductions as a setting for a collection of nineteenth-century furniture and bric-a-brac that brings the period back to life in a charming way.

An adjacent building, The Cottage, was recently added to the inn. Built in 1873 for the coal baron's son, it is a delightful empire style home with bright airy rooms furnished with choice antiques.

Croquet on the lawn, with the men wearing straw boaters; afternoon tea on the porch, including the hosts leading stimulating conversation

Left, everyone enjoys croquet as much as porch sitting. Above, a tour de force of Victorian decoration.

THE QUEEN VICTORIA

Imposing Victorian on Cape May

The Queen Victoria ranks among the best of Cape May's many distinctive bed and breakfast inns. It towers on the corner of Ocean Street and Columbia Avenue, a dramatic green and maroon gingerbread cottage. Owners Joan and Dane Wells are perfectly suited to the task of pampering this Victorian lady. Before beginning a career as an innkeeper, Joan was curator of the Molly Brown House in Denver as well as the executive director of The Victorian Society. Both positions required a dedication to the preservation of old houses, a labor Joan truly loves. Dan is the perfect counterpart. Though a tinkerer and hardware store aficionado, his professional background in retailing keeps the inn's business side on an even keel.

One of the most attractive and interesting rooms in the entire house is the front parlor, which is filled with the Wellses' Arts and Crafts furniture collection—that wonderfully subdued offspring of the gaudy Victorian age.

Bedrooms come in many shapes and sizes. On the first floor the Queen Victoria room handily houses a massive armoire, tufted couch, king-size bed, and petit point chairs. Several rooms on the second floor and all on the third are diminutive and charming. The Wellses carefully selected wallpapers to suit the spirit of Victoriana, each with jewel-like hues and intricate patterns.

Though Cape May is a wonderful place to visit, no matter the season, the Wellses favorite time of year is Christmas. To make the season more joyous, they organize caroling, fireside readings from Dickens, and workshop sessions devoted to planning the Victorian Christmas dinner and decorating the Victorian home.

THE QUEEN VICTORIA, 102 Ocean St., Cape May, NJ 08204; (609) 884-8702; Dane and Joan Wells, hosts. French and some Spanish spoken. Open all year, minimum stays vary seasonally. Eleven guest rooms and two suites, all with private baths. Rates: $75 to $120 per room, $130 to $198 per suite according to size and amenities (rates lower off season), including full breakfast served buffet style. Afternoon tea. Excellent dining nearby. Children in suites only; no pets; smoking restricted; Visa/MasterCard.

DIRECTIONS: take Garden State Pkwy. to Cape May, where it becomes Lafayette St. Turn left at second stoplight (Ocean St.) and proceed three blocks to inn, on right.

CAPTAIN MEY'S INN

Graced with exquisite detail

America's oldest seaside resort, Cape May conjures by its very name, visions of gingerbread and wedding-cake castles-by-the-sea. Protected from progress by the Pine Barrens and acres of wetlands plus miles of fertile fields that yield succulent Jersey produce, the village retains much of the charm of centuries past.

One advantage for today's visitor is the abundance of lovely bed and breakfast establishments, each quite different in spirit and temperament. The three on these pages are a sampler; it would take weeks to exhaust all the possibilities.

Captain Mey's Inn is named for Cornelius Jacobsen Mey, of the Dutch East Indies Company, who explored the area in 1621 and served as its namesake. This solidly built, late-Victorian mansion is decorated like an old-fashioned valentine. Voluminous lace curtains and lacey privacy screens,

Two details of the foyer and parlor.

called *horretjes*, frame the windows. A china cabinet filled with innkeeper Carin Fedderman's collection of antique Delftware, family portraits, a nineteenth-century bible, antique pewter and copper, and abundant knickknacks and bric-a-brac fill the first-floor parlor and dining room. Carin is from Holland, and her Dutch heritage, linked with that of Captain Mey, inspired her and partner Milly La Canfora to create an inn reminiscent of her home. Many small touches—a small Persian rug on the clawfoot dining table; a plush, purse-like tea cozy; and the decorative *horretjes*—are found in many Dutch homes and add a distinctive European flavor. The house itself is graced with exquisite detail from three signed Tiffany stained-glass windows in the inner foyer to leaded, diamond-paned, ripple glass windows that glisten in the wide bay in the dining room.

CAPTAIN MEY'S INN, 202 Ocean St., Cape May, NJ 08204; (609) 884-7793/9637; Carin Fedderman and Milly La Canfora, hostesses. Dutch spoken and some French, German, Spanish, Italian. Open all year, weekends only January through March. Nine guest rooms, private and shared baths. Rates $60 to $125 double, varying with season and amenities; includes full breakfast served by candlelight. Afternoon tea. Excellent dining nearby. Children over ten; no pets; smoking restricted to the veranda; Visa/MasterCard; parking available. Cape May offers beaches (beach passes available), sight-seeing, antiques.

DIRECTIONS: take causeway bridge (Lafayette St.) to second light and turn left onto Ocean St. Inn is 1½ blocks ahead.

A Dutch tea cozy.

Left, the dining room, furnished in impeccable Victorian style.

THE MAINSTAY INN

Bed and breakfast at its best

The heyday of Cape May as one of the premier resort towns on the East Coast coincided with the height of Victorian carpenter craftsmanship in the latter part of the nineteenth century, and Cape May has hundreds of finely crafted, exquisitely detailed gingerbread houses to prove it.

One of these, an Italianate former gaming house built in 1872, was restored to its former glory by Tom and Sue Carroll, who have made the Mainstay into the best known bed and breakfast in the East. Because of their painstaking search for authenticity in the recreation of Victorian interiors, their inn has become a highly respected and much-loved model for other innkeepers aspiring to recreate the same sort of ambiance.

The interior of the inn is a unique combination of lush, Persian and Oriental rugs, wonderfully decorative Bradbury and Bradbury period wallpapers and mouldings, elaborate details in the form of paintings, china, drapes, lamps, quilts, chandeliers, clocks, vases, and, finally, an overwhelming collection of Victorian antique furniture. Guest rooms contain giant beds with decorative foot and head boards, intricately carved wardrobes, dressers, and washstands with marble tops, and velvet upholstered chairs and settees. The public rooms contain more: giant pier mirrors, elaborately upholstered walnut and mahogany chairs and settees, and exotic divans.

Amidst this Victorian flamboyance, the perfectly modern young innkeepers maintain an air of calm and serenity throughout the two guest houses. Guests meet each other over the delicious full breakfasts and during afternoon tea, oftentimes served on the Mainstay's ample porch.

THE MAINSTAY INN, 635 Columbia Avenue, Cape May, NJ 08204; (609) 884-8690; Tom and Sue Carroll, hosts. Open mid-March through mid-December. Twelve rooms, all with private baths, Rates: $95 to $120 per couple in season; includes full breakfast and afternoon tea. No liquor served; guests may bring their own. Children over 12 welcome; no pets; smoking on veranda only; no credit cards. Croquet and swimming at the seashore are popular activities.

DIRECTIONS: 2 blocks from Convention Hall in the center of town.

MARYLAND

WHITE SWAN TAVERN

Stay the night in a comfortable museum

Three and one half years of preparation went into the making of the White Swan Tavern, and the effect is that of a comfortable museum. The original section of the building dates back to the early 1700s when John Lovegrove operated a tannery on the site. Over the years the property changed hands and became a tavern that offered accommodations to travelers. In 1977, Horace Havemeyer, Jr., bought the property. Before beginning the restoration, he undertook exhaustive historical research and an archeological dig. Artifacts and shards of pottery, including a serving dish (a 1730 North Devon charger) that has been beautifully reproduced as the inn's china, are on display in a backlit wall case.

A stay at the White Swan is rewarding because guests can feel the care the inn has been given. The main floor contains three parlors, or sitting rooms. The formal and dignified Joseph Nicholson Room, named after the second owner of the property, is furnished from Mr. Nicholson's inventory, a document unearthed during research. The Isaac Cannell Room is filled with game tables appropriate to the days when it was an integral part of the original tavern.

Bedrooms are decorated in several styles. Three are done in formal colonial: one with pencil post twin beds, one with a lace canopied double bed, and one with cannonball four-posters. All have wing chairs for reading, fresh colors, and beautiful hardwood floors. The T.W. Elliason Suite, added to the tavern at the turn-of-the-century, has been restored to its Victorian origins. This bedroom and separate sitting room are decorated with high-back massive beds, a tufted settee, decorative friezes, and a busy floral carpet. A unique color scheme of golds, greens, copper, and peach is vibrant and true to the era. The final bedchamber is located in the oldest section of the structure. Named Lovegrove's Kitchen because it was the site of its namesake's tannery, this rustic suite has an original beam ceiling, brick floor, wide

Above, the old kitchen serves as a guest room.

The King Joseph Room, a private sitting room for guests, above.

In the winter the inn is filled with dried flowers.

kitchen hearth, and is accented with homespun blue-and-cream curtains and bedspreads, antique tables, and a wing chair for reading.

The White Swan's continental breakfast is special because it employs the talents of a gifted local baker and includes fresh-squeezed orange juice and grapefruit juice. Served in the Isaac Cannell Room, guests may request that breakfast be delivered to their door instead.

Chestertown, an important seaport in the early 1700s, is one of those special American towns that still reflects its moment of prosperity. The seat of Kent County and the home of Washington College, the town retains a great measure of grace and atmosphere.

WHITE SWAN TAVERN, 231 High St., Chestertown, MD 21620; (301) 778-2300; Mary S. Clarkson, hostess. Closed two weeks per year (usually early February). Six guest rooms in house, one attached "summer kitchen" suite, all private baths. Rates: $75 to $100, double occupancy; $25 per extra occupant; rates include light breakfast. Good dining nearby, especially in season. Children welcome; no pets; no credit cards. Area offers local museums, walking tours, recreation, wildlife preserves.

DIRECTIONS: from Chesapeake Bay Bridge (Rte. 50-301), take Rte. 301N to Rte. 213. Turn left on Rte. 213 to Chestertown, approx. 15 miles. Cross the Chester River Bridge and turn left at first stop light (Cross St.). Turn left again at next light (High St.). Inn is in middle of block on right. From north, take Rte. 301S to Rte. 544. Proceed on 544 to stop light and turn left. Pass college and turn right at second light (Cross St.) Proceed as above.

THE TAVERN HOUSE

A village focus for 200 years

The ebb and flow of history has left an indelible mark on Vienna, a village anchored securely on the banks of the Nanticoke River, which meanders across Maryland's benevolent Eastern Shore. As one of the oldest settlements in Maryland, part of a land grant to Lord Baltimore and dating back to 1664, it was once a prosperous shipbuilding and tobacco-growing town. Vienna was raided by the British during the American Revolution and was fired on by the British during the War of 1812—just two of many significant moments in the life of this town.

The Tavern House has been a focal point in Vienna since the 18th century. Although the exact date of its construction is unknown, the first innkeeper on record, Alexander Laing, opened these doors to travelers in the 1760s. Besides innkeeping duties, throughout the ensuing decades Tavern House innkeepers had the responsibility of ferrying people, to and fro, across the Nanticoke.

Innkeepers Harvey and Elise Altergott don't pilot a ferry, but they are successfully continuing the tradition of hospitality established by their predecessors and they will pick up visitors who fly into one of the surrounding local airports. To

everyone who walks through their door it is immediately apparent that the Altergotts take great pleasure in greeting strangers, and this sense of good cheer is contagious.

These innkeepers are also committed to preserving the simple and elegant seventeenth-century character of their inn. They had original paint chips analyzed in order to exactly match the eighteenth and nineteenth-century tints that were used throughout the interior of the house; they had locks fabricated to duplicate the outline found on the doors; and they replastered with a colonial concoction of lime, sand, and hair. Each room in the inn is simply and comfortably furnished with antiques, handmade reproductions, and traditional pieces that live well with this historic gem of an inn.

THE TAVERN HOUSE, 111 Water Street, P.O. Box 98, Vienna, MD 21869; (301) 376-3347; Harvey and Elise Altergott, hosts. Open all year. Four rooms sharing 2 baths. Rates: $45 to $55 single; $50 to $60 double, with "special" full breakfast. Children over 12 welcome; no pets; Visa/MasterCard accepted; Spanish, German spoken. Area has tennis, boating, and birdwatching in the Blackwater Wildlife Refuge. Chesapeake Bay seafood restaurants abound in area.

DIRECTIONS: situated on Maryland's Eastern Shore of Chesapeake Bay, half way between Salisbury and Cambridge on Rte. 50.

The inn's formal front parlor, looking into the living-dining room.

THE ROSEBUD INN

Return to another time

When a body wearies of the daily grind and longs to escape to a simpler life, to a place where time seems to stand still, the village of Woodsboro awaits.

Once you arrive, the place to hang your hat is the Rosebud Inn, a solidly comfortable and immaculate guest house. The inn is owned by Alice and Albert Eaton, ex-city folk who fell in love with Woodsboro's bucolic charm and never turned back.

From the outside, the Rosebud is a solid, red brick, Colonial Revival home, with a wide, wraparound veranda supported by classical Ionic columns. The house was built in 1920 by Woodsboro's most prominent citizen, Dr. George F. Smith, founder of the Rosebud Perfume Company, which remains in operation next door to the inn, manufacturing rose-scented salve in sweet little tins. It is inside, however, where one truly appreciates the inn, for the physician spared no expense, installing marble and slate fireplaces, glistening oak floors inlaid with maple and walnut;

fine woodwork; oak paneling; and stained glass windows bearing the likeness of his beloved rose.

The Eatons have renovated and refurbished the house to a gleaming finish. Each guest bedroom is beautifully appointed, and the Eatons have added many small touches that make one feel thoroughly at home.

THE ROSEBUD INN, 4 North Main Street, Woodsboro, MD 21798; (301) 845-2221; Albert and Alice Eaton, hosts. Open all year. Six rooms and one cottage share 5 bathrooms. Rates: $60 to $65 double with continental breakfast. Children over 6 welcome; no pets; Visa/MasterCard accepted; German spoken. Tennis, swimming, boating, fishing, riding, antiquing nearby. Three country restaurants within walking distance.

DIRECTIONS: from I-70, I-270, or I-340 take U.S. 15 north 3 miles past Frederick to Rte. 26 East and turn right to Rte. 194. Left for 6 miles on 194 to Woodsboro and inn.

The Dining Room's woodwork and detailing is original to the house.

One of the restored parlors.

SPRING BANK INN

The rebirth of a stylish rural home

In 1880 gentleman farmer George Houck spared no expense when he built the most stylish home rural Frederick County had ever seen. Constructed of red brick, the house was given a Gothic Revival bay window, columned veranda, and gabled, fish-scale patterned slate roof. It was further embellished with elegant Italianate windows and an ornate belvedere for viewing the beautiful vistas of the surrounding countryside.

A century later the house captured the imaginations of Beverly and Ray Compton, who noticed it while on a bicycle tour of the area. Captivated as well by the rich history and architectural charms of Frederick, they soon bought Spring Bank Farm and embarked on a massive and much-needed restoration. Since the Comptons open bedrooms to overnight guests as each room

is completed, today's guests are attending the birth of an inn and the rebirth of a house, with such fine details as frescoed ceilings, original brass hardware, louvered shutters, hand-marbled slate fireplaces, and hand-grained woodwork revealing themselves in the process.

Ray's family has been in the antiques business for several decades, and this expertise shows in many of Spring Bank's furnishings. High-ceilinged bedrooms easily accommodate full Victorian bedroom sets, canopied beds, and easy chairs. Plans are in the works to convert the third floor, which gives access to the belvedere, into an antiques shop.

SPRING BANK INN, 7945 Worman's Mill Rd., Frederick, MD 21701; (301) 694-0440; Beverly and Ray Compton, hosts. Elegant 1880 rural home that combines Greek Revival and Italiante architecture. Open year-round. Seven guest rooms, one with private bath. Rates $60–70 single, $70–80 double. Hearty continental breakfast. No children under twelve; no pets; no smoking in home; American Express/checks. Appalachian trail close by; trout fishing; historic district to explore. Wide range of good restaurants in town.

DIRECTIONS: from I-70, I-270, or 340, take U.S. 15 north about 5 miles, driving past Frederick. Look for "mile 16" marker; turn right at next road onto Rte. 355 south. Inn is ¼ mile south on left.

PHOTOGRAPHS COURTESY NATIONAL PIKE INN

NATIONAL PIKE INN

In the antiques capital of Maryland

"We're here and available," says Terry Rimel. "We give our guests as much hospitality as they want." At the National Pike Inn you can play the parlor organ, have breakfast in bed, and feel like a part of the family.

Conveniently located between Baltimore and Frederick, New Market has been dubbed the "Antiques Capitol of Maryland." More than forty antiques stores lure the collector here to shops specializing in folk art, clocks, early lighting, porcelain, jewelry, and Victorian furniture. "New Market Days" in the fall celebrate the town's heritage, and early December is aglow with traditional Christmas decorations, music makers, and shops stuffed with gifts.

The guest rooms in the inn are air conditioned and provide fresh flowers and fruit. The Victorian Room has a four poster covered with a rosebud and mint-green chintz spread, a green tapestry Victorian settee, a Cheval mirror, and carved cherry wood dresser. The Canopy Room has steps leading up to its canopied bed, a chenille spread, a piecrust table, and fireside bench.

A courtyard in the back has a privacy fence permitting quiet sunning in the azalea garden, with its ornate bird bath. A screened-in side porch looks out on a fountain. For those venturing further afield there is touring and tasting at two local wineries, and the Catoctin Mountains and Cunningham Falls are forty-five minutes away.

NATIONAL PIKE INN, 9–11 Main Street, P.O. Box 299, New Market, MD 21774; (301) 865-5055; Tom and Terry Rimel, hosts. Open all year. Five guest rooms with private and shared baths (suite available). Rates: $60 to $100 includes continental plus breakfast. Special weekly rates and on stays over two nights. Children over five; no pets; smoking permitted; Visa/MasterCard.

DIRECTIONS: from I-70 take exit 62 to Rte. 75 and go north 1 block to Main St. Take left on Main St. (Rte. 144) for about 3 blocks to top of hill to inn in center of town.

The richness and warmth of the parlor.

SOCIETY HILL HOPKINS

Four periods to choose from

The first room you notice is the charming parlor with its floral couch and matching wallpaper border, faux-finish mantel, etched glass Victorian chandelier, handsome artworks, and lace panel curtains. Guests often relax here with a cup of coffee or a glass of sherry.

The twenty-six guest rooms in this Spanish revival building have been arranged into four different periods: Federal, Victorian, Art Deco, and Contemporary. Guests are invited to reserve that period room that suits their mood or sense of fantasy.

Gray, lavender, peach, and blue offset the patterned rugs in the Federal room. The wallpaper border is a classical Adams frieze, and the mahogany armoire, Chippendale-style chairs, draped valances, and old prints enhance the period effect.

The Victorian room features a dressing mirror, wicker desk, white iron sweetheart bedstead, marble-topped tables, and lace curtains, while the Art Deco room has black lacquer furniture, Chinese-style lamps, twenties prints, and touches of period maroons and greys.

Finally, the contemporary room in browns and persimmon, accented in green, has a bed with brass headboard, rattan night stands, a pine armoire, and Hitchcock-style chair.

The monotony of the usual assemblage of small hotel rooms will not be found here; appointments do not smack of the decorator's art. Instead the charm of European bed and breakfasts and the warm hospitality of American country inns combines in a uniquely exciting blend.

SOCIETY HILL HOPKINS, 3404 St. Paul Street, Baltimore, MD 21218; (301) 235-8600; Joanne Fritz, innkeeper. A historic building in a historic neighborhood. Open year-round. Twenty-six guest rooms, including suites, all with private baths; some with kitchenettes. Rates: $90–$130. Continental breakfast. Children welcome; no pets; smoking permitted; major credit cards accepted. Within walking distance of Baltimore Museum of Art, one block from John Hopkins University.
DIRECTIONS: call for directions.

SOCIETY HILL GOVERNMENT HOUSE

Baltimore's official bed and breakfast

These adjoining historic townhouses have been completely renovated and refurbished into Baltimore's premier bed and breakfast establishment. The project was the brainchild of the dynamic mayor, William Donald Schaefer. Painstakingly researched for historical accuracy, the complex was worked on for three years before it could offer hospitality in the style and manner for which Baltimore is noted. Swathed in Bradbury and Bradbury wallpaper, bedecked in Scalamandré and Schumacher fabrics, and outfitted with both antiques and fine reproductions, this grande dame has never appeared more glamorous.

The décor of the guest rooms, clearly influenced by the Federal period, reflects a traditional Baltimore style. Sitting areas in guest rooms offer a table and desk and TV. Guests choose from one of two continental breakfasts brought to their room at a specified time.

In addition to providing hospitality to bed and breakfast guests, the house often hosts official government functions in the splendid library, reception hall, and dining room. His Honor, the mayor, maintains an elegant suite for accommodating dignitaries, such as the Mayor of Rotterdam.

Another function performed here is the training of small groups of unemployed area citizens as housekeepers, bartenders, hostesses, and waiters to satisfy Baltimore's burgeoning need for hospitality services.

Historically correct and graciously managed, the Society Hill Government House is a premier bed and breakfast serving Baltimore and the greater community—yet another jewel in Baltimore's crown.

SOCIETY HILL GOVERNMENT HOUSE, 1125-1129 N. Calvert Street, Baltimore, MD 21202; (301) 752-7722; Deborah Fischer, innkeeper. Open year-round. Eighteen guest rooms, all with private bath and individual heating and cooling systems. Rates: $90–$110. Continental breakfast included. Children welcome; no pets; smoking permitted; major credit cards accepted.
DIRECTIONS: call for directions.

TWIN GATES B & B

Hospitality in north Baltimore

Twin Gates was built in 1857 as the home of Benjamin Sadtler, the first principal of the Lutherville Female Seminary. Befitting his exalted station in this proper, north Baltimore community, the home, with its fashionable Second Empire styling, was among the finest in the village.

More than a century later, Gwen and Bill Vaughn stumbled into innkeeping on their way to refurbishing the house, still the most prominent home in the historic enclave of Lutherville. One of the Vaughns' daughters pointed out to her parents their joint innkeeping credentials: skill at renovation and decorating; an abiding love of people; and deftness in the kitchen. Luckily for travelers to the area, they took her advice and the outcome is an oasis of warmth, good cheer, and homey comfort.

The inn is only fifteen minutes north of Balti-

Just a few minute's drive from Baltimore's fabulous inner harbor.

more's exciting Inner Harbor, but it seems a world removed. The surrounding grounds are lush, expansive, and private. The Vaughns decorated the house using a palette of soft blue, peach, cream, and beige. The first-floor common rooms, with fourteen-foot ceilings, feel spacious, and the inn's old-fashioned front porch, furnished with white wicker and bedecked with the flags of the U.S. and Maryland, provide an added dimension of charm and comfort.

Gwen shines in the kitchen each morning, concocting such delectibles as strawberry shortcake or peach-and-orange-drenched French toast, known as "fuzzy navel." Early evening finds Bob in charge of the wine and cheese hour, during which guests recuperate from the rigors of the day, enjoy relaxed conversation, and plan an evening outing.

TWIN GATES BED & BREAKFAST, 308 Morris Avenue, Lutherville, MD 21093; (301) 252-3131; Gwen and Bob Vaughan, hosts. Open all year. Seven rooms, 3 with private baths, 4 share 2 baths. Rates: $70 to $90, with lavish, full breakfast and bedside snack. Children over 12 welcome; no pets; no credit cards; checks accepted. Flower gardens on premises. Tennis and cycling in area. Baltimore area famous for seafood restaurants.

DIRECTIONS: call for specific details, depending on which direction you are coming from.

Second-floor bedroom has a private balcony overlooking the rear garden.

WASHINGTON, D.C.

DUPONT CIRCLE

A cosmopolitan part of Washington

The tree-lined streets of Dupont Circle house quite a grand array of Victorian mansions—many of which serve as embassies, clubs, or institutions such as the National Trust for Historic Preservation. The neighborhood is cosmopolitan and its shopping district is known for an inviting assemblage of specialty shops, bookstores, cafés, and pubs.

A third-floor bedroom in the turret, shown in the photograph above.

This hewn-stone Victorian mansion is among the handsomest in the area, and it sits just two blocks from Daniel Chester French's statue of Samuel Francis Dupont, which marks the circle. Here also is found the beginning of the shopping district, as well as a handy subway station. The house itself offers five comfortable guest bedrooms, with amenities such as televisions and bathrobes. In fact, this elegant bed and breakfast feels more like an intimate hotel than a private home.

DUPONT CIRCLE. Open all year. Five rooms, 2 with private baths and 3 sharing. Rates: $75 to $90 double with continental breakfast. No children; no pets; Visa/MasterCard/American Express. Good restaurants right across the street and in area. *Available through Bed 'N' Breakfast Ltd., Washington, D.C.*

KALORAMA GUEST HOUSE

A cosmopolitan clientele from around the world

Hidden away from the bustle of the city on a quiet residential street, the Kalorama Guest House is a home away from home. Its thirty-one well appointed rooms are put together with a cozy mix of fine antiques and grandmother's attic that includes beautiful Victorian bedsteads, armoires, and old Singer sewing machines that have been converted to tables.

PHOTOGRAPHS BY MICHAEL ACH

Wrought iron park benches serve as seating for breakfast in the brick-walled dining room.

Vintage photographs, old advertising prints, and portraits decorate the walls, and vases of fresh flowers lend fragrance and color to the public rooms. A generous continental breakfast is served in the brick-walled dining room where wrought iron park benches beside marble top tables afford guests from around the world the opportunity to meet and converse. Friendships can be furthered sipping afternoon sherry before a crackling fire.

Holidays are taken seriously here with a party at Halloween, stockings hung in guest rooms at Christmas, and baskets delivered to all at Easter. The fun-loving staff is attentive, friendly, and always ready to help with directions for sightseeing or museum going. Located in the Adams Morgan section, a vibrant neighborhood of old townhouses, antiques shops, and ethnic restaurants, the Kalorama is a five-minute taxi ride from downtown and all that Washington has to offer.

THE KALORAMA GUEST HOUSE at Kalorama Park, 1854 Mintwood Place, N.W., Washington, DC 20009; (202) 667-6369; Rick Fenstemaker, gen'l mgr., Tamara Wood, host. Open all year. Thirty-one rooms, some with private baths. Rates: $40 to $95, with full continental breakfast and afternoon sherry. There are no provisions for small children; no pets; checks, major credit cards accepted; smoking permitted. Limited parking space may be reserved in advance for $4 per night. Over 50 ethnic restaurants to choose from in a 2 block radius.

DIRECTIONS: from Baltimore south on I-95, take the beltway 495 west toward Silver Spring to exit 33. South on Connecticut Avenue towards Chevy Chase. Pass the zoo entrance in the 3000 block and count 4 stop lights and turn left on Calvert St. Go to 2nd stop light and turn right on Columbia; 2 blocks down turn right on Mintwood.

Noteworthy architectural details highlight a substantial old building.

Left, sherry is served in the gracious public rooms.

Left, an elaborate sculpture lights the stairway. Above, some of the art nouveau collection.

LOGAN CIRCLE

Extravagantly restored

Extensively restored by two loving owners, this one-hundred-year-old Victorian mansion features original wood paneling, stained-glass niches, ornate chandeliers, and a Victorian-style lattice porch and gardens. A mecca for lovers of "Art Nouveau," its walls are covered with highly selective and artfully framed posters, prints, magazine covers, and advertising art. The hostess, a tireless collector, is constantly adding new pieces to her collection.

In addition to the house's own beautiful appointments, the owners have incorporated some Victorian gems rescued by architectural salvagers: gilded mirrors, intricately carved mantels, and glistening English tiles. Floral patterns combine with silks, violet walls, wainscoting, draperies, oriental rugs, Eastlake furniture, and vintage floors, creating a romantic ambiance. One of two parlors houses a working player piano with silk-fringed turquoise shawl.

Each of the five guest rooms is singular and charming. An additional ground floor apartment offers complete privacy and comfort. Guest room furnishings include antique quilts, wicker, greenery, shutters, wash bowls, a Jacobean desk, and a four poster bed.

Overlooking a fountain and rose arbor, the latticed porch seduces with a promise to banish worldly cares. Here one can effortlessly return to the romance and elegance of by-gone days.

LOGAN CIRCLE. Century-old Victorian mansion with gardens, terrace, and Victorian-style lattice porch. Open year-round. Five guest rooms, with shared baths; apartment with private bath. Rates: $50-$60 single, $60-$70 double, apartment $60 single, $70 double. Continental breakfast included. Children welcome; no pets; smoking permitted; MasterCard/Visa/American Express. Logan Circle is an area in transition; guests are advised to drive rather than walk at night. *Represented by Bed 'n Breakfast Ltd. of Washington, D.C.*

FRIENDSHIP HEIGHTS

Comfort and privacy

Custom designed by its owners five years ago, this Federal-style brick house has an enclosed garden and heated pool. The pool, uncommon to most houses in the district, offers a happy solution to Washington's steamy summers.

Plush carpeting, dark woods, Chinoiserie, and a potted palm enrich the dining room, where a generous buffet breakfast is laid.

The guest room on the lower level, with a working fireplace, is next to a game room outfitted with a pool table, pinball machine, working Victorola, and exercise bike. The guest room on the upper level is next to a sitting room with an interesting assortment of books, TV, and potted palm.

FRIENDSHIP HEIGHTS. Federal-style brick house. Open year-round. Two guest rooms, each with private bath. Rates: $55 single, $65 double. Expanded continental breakfast included. Children accepted; no pets; smoking downstairs only; MasterCard/Visa/American Express. Metro is ten-minute walk. *Represented by Bed 'n Breakfast Ltd. of Washington, D.C.*

Looking onto the sun porch.

CHEVY CHASE

Antiques-filled modern townhouse

The owners of this splendid contemporary townhouse make guests feel as if they are in their own home. During the week, visitors may prepare their own breakfast, if they wish, and afterward sun themselves on the private patio or bicycle through the adjoining park. The displays of Spanish art and a magnificent collection of Lladró figurines are complemented by fine antique furnishings.

CHEVY CHASE. Spacious, English-style townhouse in townhouse community. Open year-round. Rates $50 single, $55 double. Full breakfast, prepared by guests during the week. Well-behaved pets only. In Chevy Chase, Maryland; all of Washington is accessible by car. *Represented by Sweet Dreams & Toast, Inc. Washington, DC.*

BED & BREAKFAST RESERVATION AGENCIES

The concept of Bed and Breakfast in the United States is rapidly expanding. To facilitate this phenomenon, reservation agencies are quickly cropping up, resulting in rapidly changing information. Many of the agencies listed below have been in existence for some time; others have been organized recently. Do not be surprised if there are changes when you contact them.

*Only a selection of agencies are listed here. Complete information can be obtained from **Bed and Breakfast Reservation Services Worldwide**, P.O. Box 14797, Dept 174, Baton Rouge, LA 70898.*

Connecticut

ALEXANDER'S BED AND BREAKFAST RESERVATION SERVICE, Route 44 East, Salisbury, CT 06068; (203) 435-9539; Doris and Dick Alexander. A Variety of homestays in the *Berkshire Mountains of Connecticut, Massachusetts, and New York.*

BED AND BREAKFAST, LTD., P.O. Box 216, New Haven, CT 06513; (203) 469-3260; Jack Argenio. Write, sending SASE, or call between 5–9 P.M. weekdays and any time weekends. Period homes, estates, farms. *125 listings statewide.*

COVERED BRIDGE BED & BREAKFAST, P.O. Box 447, Norfolk, CT 06058; (203) 542-5944; Diane Trembay. *Northwest Connecticut, southern Berkshires, Hudson Valley, and Connecticut shoreline.*

NUTMEG BED AND BREAKFAST AGENCY, 222 Girard Avenue, Hartford, CT 06105; (203) 236-6698; Maxine Kates. 9:30 A.M. to 5 P.M. Monday through Friday. Vacation homes, restored historic homes, relocation. *Connecticut.*

District of Columbia

THE BED & BREAKFAST LEAGUE/SWEET DREAMS & TOAST, P.O. Box 9490, Washington, DC 20016; (202) 363-7767; Millie Groobey. *Washington, D.C., and adjacent suburbs.*

BED 'N' BREAKFAST LTD. OF WASHINGTON, D.C., P.O. Box 12011, Washington, DC 20005; (202) 328-3510; Jackie Reed and Lisa Stofan. *Washington metropolitan areas, specializing in the historic districts.*

Maine

BED & BREAKFAST DOWN EAST LTD., Macomber Mill Road, Box 547, Eastbrook, ME 04634; (207) 565-3517; Sally Godfrey. Private homes at lakeside, countryside, town, or coast. *Maine.*

BED & BREAKFAST OF MAINE, 32 Colonial Village, Falmouth, ME 04105; (207) 781-4528; Peg Tierney. Weekdays 6–11 P.M.; weekends 10 A.M. to 10 P.M. *Coastal Maine and nearby islands.*

Maryland

AMANDA'S BED & BREAKFAST RESERVATION SERVICE, 1428 Park Avenue, Baltimore, MD 21217; (301) 225-0001; Betsy Grater. 9:00 A.M. to 5:00 P.M. weekdays. Private homes and small inns. *Baltimore, Annapolis, Eastern shore of Maryland, and Western Maryland.*

THE TRAVELLER IN MARYLAND, 33 West Street, Annapolis, MD 21401; (301) 269-6232, 261-2233; Cecily Sharp-Whitehill. 9 A.M. to 5 P.M. Monday to Thursday; 9 A.M. to noon Friday. Yachts, inns, private homes. *Maryland, London, Paris.*

Massachusetts

BED AND BREAKFAST ASSOCIATES, Bay Colony, Ltd., P.O. Box 166, Babson Park Branch, Boston, MA 02157; (617) 449-5302; Arline Kardasis. *Eastern Massachusetts.*

BED AND BREAKFAST BROOKLINE/BOSTON, Box 732, Brookline, MA 02146; (617) 277-2292; Anne Diamond. 10 A.M. to 4 P.M. Victorian townhouses and Beacon Hill homes. *Boston/Brookline, Cambridge, Cape Cod, Nantucket, Plymouth, Gloucester.*

BED AND BREAKFAST A LÀ CAMBRIDGE AND GREATER BOSTON, P.O. Box 665, Cambridge, MA 02140; (617) 576-1492; Pamela Carruthers. 9 A.M. to 6 P.M. Monday–Friday; 10 A.M. to 3 P.M. Saturday. Private and vacation homes of every description. *Boston, Cambridge, Lexington, and Concord areas.*

BED AND BREAKFAST CAPE COD, Box 341, West Hyannisport, MA 02672; (617) 775-2772; Clark Diehl. Country inns, sea captains' houses, host homes. *Cape Cod, Martha's Vineyard, Nantucket, Gloucester, and Cape Ann.*

BERKSHIRE BED AND BREAKFAST HOMES, P.O. Box 211, Williamsburg, MA 01096; (413) 268-7244; Eleanor Hebert. *Private homes in western Mass. from Sturbridge to the Berkshires.*

HOST HOMES OF BOSTON, P.O. Box 117, Waban Branch, Boston, MA 02168; (617) 244-1308; Marcia Whittington. *Covers Boston and select city suburbs.*

PINEAPPLE HOSPITALITY, INC., 384 Rodney French Blvd., New Bedford, MA 02744; (508) 990-1696; Joan Brownhill. 9 A.M. to 6 P.M. weekdays. Homes or small inns. *Six-state area of New England.*

New Hampshire

NEW HAMPSHIRE BED & BREAKFAST, RFD 3, Box 53, Laconia, NH 03246; (603) 279-8348; Martha Dorais. Country classics, waterfront, mountain views, farms. *New Hampshire.*

New Jersey

BED & BREAKFAST OF NEW JERSEY, INC., Suite 132, 103 Godwin Avenue, Midland Park, NJ 07432; (201) 444-7409; Aster Mould. Vacation homes, refurbished mansions, apartments. *New Jersey, including seashore, and Delaware River area. Package tours.*

New York

ABODE BED & BREAKFAST, LTD., P.O. Box 20022, New York, NY 10028; (212) 472-2000; Shelly Leifer. *Manhattan and Brooklyn Heights.*

ALTERNATE LODGINGS INC., P.O. Box 1782, East Hampton, L.I., NY 11937; (516) 324-9449; Francine and Robert Hauxwell. *The Hamptons from Westhampton to Montauk Point.*

THE AMERICAN COUNTRY COLLECTION, 984 Gloucester Place, Schenectady, NY 12309; (518) 370-4948; Beverly Walsh. *Northeastern New York, Vermont, Western Massachusetts.*

A REASONABLE ALTERNATIVE, INC., 117 Spring Street, Port Jefferson, NY 11777; (516) 928-4034; Kathleen Dexter. *Long Island along the North and South shores of Nassau and Suffolk Counties.*

BED AND BREAKFAST (& BOOKS), 35 West 92nd Street, New York, NY 10025; (212) 865-8740; Judith Goldberg. A unique service offering a selection of hosts who work as photographers, psychologists, lawyers, dancers, teachers, and artists, with special knowledge of New York's rich cultural life. *New York City.*

BED & BREAKFAST U.S.A., LTD., P.O. Box 606, Croton-on-Hudson, NY 10520; (914) 271-6228; Barbara Notarius and Doris Tomer (Albany region rep. (518) 273-1851). *New York City, New York State, Great Britain, France, Canada, New Zealand.*

CITY LIGHTS LTD., P.O. Box 20355, Cherokee Station, New York, NY 10028; (212) 737-7049; Dee Staff and Davida Rosenblum. 9:00 A.M. to 5:00 P.M. Monday to Friday; 9:00 A.M. to 12:00 P.M. Saturday. Hosted and unhosted apartments from studios to four bedrooms in apartment houses and brownstones. Two night minimum stay. *Manhattan, Park Slope, Brooklyn Heights, and Queens.*

NEW WORLD BED AND BREAKFAST, 150 Fifth Avenue, Suite 711, New York, NY 10011; (800) 443-3800; (212) 675-5600 (for calls from within New York state); Laura Tilden. 9:30 A.M. to 5 P.M. Monday to Friday. Hosted and unhosted apartments in high rises, brownstones, and carriage houses. Two night minimum stay. *Manhattan.*

NORTH COUNTRY BED & BREAKFAST RESERVATION SERVICE, Box 286, Lake Placid, NY 12946; (518) 523-9474; Lyn Witte. 11 A.M. to 8 P.M. daily. Private homes, country inns, and mountain resorts. *The Adirondack Mountains from Glens Falls north to the Canadian border, and from Lake Champlain west to Watertown.*

RAINBOW HOSPITALITY BED AND BREAKFAST, 758 Richmond Avenue, Buffalo, NY 14222; (716) 283-4794 or 881-9977; Georgia Brannan and Cheryl Biggie. *Rochester, Niagara Falls, and Buffalo areas.*

URBAN VENTURES, INC., P.O. Box 426, New York, NY 10024; (212) 594-5650; Mary McAulay. *Manhattan and other boroughs.*

Pennsylvania

BED & BREAKFAST CENTER CITY, 1804 Pine Street, Philadelphia, PA 19103; (215) 735-1137; Karen and Gordon Andresen. *Philadelphia's Center City, Rittenhouse Square, Antique Row, Society Hill, University City, Art Museum area.*

HERSHEY BED & BREAKFAST RESERVATION SERVICE, P.O. Box 208, Hershey, PA 17033; (717) 533-2928; Renee Deutel. Call from 10 A.M. to 3 P.M. *Lebanon and Hershey.*

BED & BREAKFAST OF PHILADELPHIA, P.O. Box 630, Chester Springs, PA 19425; (215) 827-9650; Betsy Augustine. *Philadelphia, its suburbs, and surrounding historic countryside, including Valley Forge, Chadds Ford, New Hope, and Amish countryside.*

PITTSBURGH BED & BREAKFAST, 2190 Ben Franklin Drive, Pittsburgh, PA 15237; (412) 367-8080; Judy Antico.

BED & BREAKFAST OF SOUTHEAST PENNSYLVANIA, 146 W. Philadelphia Ave., Boyertown, PA 19512; Patricia Fedor. Call anytime. Old farmhouses, restored grist mills, town and suburban houses. *Reading and Allentown area, Bethlehem, and Lancaster county.*

REST & REPAST BED & BREAKFAST SERVICE, P.O. Box 126, Pine Grove Mills, PA 16868; (814) 238-1484; Linda Feltman and Brent Peters. 9 A.M. to 12 P.M. and 6:30 P.M. to 9:30 P.M. Closed Thursday and Sunday. Farms, National Historic Register homes, apartments. *Main Penn State campus vicinity plus Huntington and Altoona areas.*

Rhode Island

CASTLE KEEP, 44 Everett Street, Newport, RI 02840; (401) 846-0362; Audrey Grimes and Dorothy Ranhofer. 8 A.M. to 8 P.M. May to Sept. Restored colonials, Victorian mini-mansions, and condos by the sea. *Newport.*

GUEST HOUSE ASSOCIATION OF NEWPORT, P.O. Box 981, Newport, RI 02840; (401) 846-7666.

Vermont

VERMONT BED & BREAKFAST, Box 139, Browns Trace, Jericho, VT 05465; (802) 899-2354; Sue and Dave Eaton. *Vermont only.*